Choosing that perfect name for your infant can be a joyous experience for you. Today's children are named after people, animals, flowers, minerals and even planets and stars. Few will criticize if you just make up a name! Look at the choices you have for every letter!

On the other hand, the whole exercise may be too huge, and you may be having trouble narrowing down those choices. "My son has to live with this name for a long time." "I don't want my child to hate his name." "But I want it to be meaningful." You may be thinking some or all of these things.

Name That Baby Boy is designed as an easy-to-use reality check to help you choose that perfect name for your perfect baby. Traditional names, unusual names, the most popular names, international names and legendary and mythical names —you'll find a melting pot of possibilities. Each name appears with its place of origin and its meaning. When a name draws from several countries, as many do, the various cultures are noted, and the meaning given reflects the standard meaning.

Don't despair if you have what you consider a simple name in mind, and you can't find it. The range of names is narrowed to include only one of the variety of names taken from the same root. For example, Alan, meaning cheerful, in harmony and of Celtic origin, represents the group of names that includes Allan, Allen and Allyn. The Where to Find list below will assist you in finding other popular names.

Where to Find ...

Alastair, Allister, Alaster	see Alexander
Bennett	see Benedict
Elvin	see Alvin
Fritz	see Frederick
Manuel	see Emmanuel
Norris	see Norman
Pedro, Pierre, Perrin, Pierce	see Peter
Rolf(e), Rolph, Rollin, Rollo	see Rudolph

Most of all, trust yourself to choose that perfect name for that perfect little boy!

—Joan C. Verniero

name that

BABY
BOY

over 3000 names
and their meanings
for your baby

written by Joan Verniero
illustrated by Kerren Barbas

The C.R.Gibson Company, Norwalk, Connecticut 06856

A

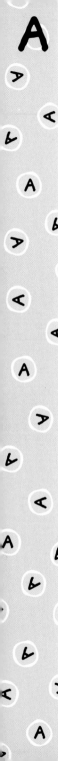

Aaron (Hebrew)
• tower of strength

Abbot (Hebrew)
• father

Abel (Hebrew)
• breath

Abner (Hebrew)
• paternal, bright

Abraham (Hebrew)
• tall, father of many

Achilles (Greek)
• hero of the Trojan War

Acton (Old English)
• of the town by the oaks

Adam (Hebrew, Phoenician)
• earth, clay, man

Adar (Syrian, Hebrew)
• ruler, prince, noble

Aidan (Hebrew)
• sensual, fire

Adlai (Hebrew)
• my ornament

Adler (German)
• eagle

Adolph (German)
• noble wolf

Adonis (Greek)
• handsome

Adrian (Latin)
• pessimistic, of the sea cost

Adriel (Hebrew)
• member of God's flock

Afton (English)
• place in England

Ahab (Hebrew)
• uncle

Aiken (Old English)
• of oak

Akar (Turkish)
• flowing stream

Akeem (Arabic)
• most wise

Aladdin (Arabic)
• height of faith

Alan (Celtic)
• cheerful, in harmony

Albert (Teutonic)
• firm, responsible, noble

Alcott (Celtic)
• of the stone cottage

Alden (Old English)
• old friend

Aldrich (Teutonic)
• king

Alexander (Greek)
• leader, defender of men

Alfonso (Spanish)
• noble, eager

Alfred (Old English)
• of good counsel, kingly

Alger (Anglo-Saxon)
• spearman

Ali (Arabic, Swahili)
• exalted

Alison (Teutonic)
• of holy fame

Aloysius (Latin)
• grace

A

Alphonse (Teutonic)
•ready for battle

Alvin (Teutonic)
•noble friend, beloved

Amadeus (Latin)
•loves God

Amal (Hebrew, Arabic)
•worker, hopeful

Ambrose (Greek)
•immortal

Amery (Teutonic)
•industrious

Amir (Arabic)
•ruler, tribal chief

Amos (Hebrew)
•strong, burden carrier

Anatole (Greek)
•of the east

Andrew (Greek)
•manly

Angelo (Greek)
•angel, messenger

Angus (Celtic)
•exceptional

Anselm (Teutonic)
•divine helmet of God

Anthony (Latin)
•incomparable, to be praised

Archibald (Teutonic)
•holy prince

Arden (Latin)
•eager, sincere

Ariel (Hebrew)
•lion of God

Aristotle (Greek)
•best

Arlen (Irish)
•pledge, oath

Armand (French)
•public spirited

Armstrong (Old English)
•with a strong arm

Arnold (Scandinavian)
•strong as an eagle

Arthur (Celtic)
•high-minded, strong as a rock

Arvin (Teutonic)
•friend of the people

Asher (Hebrew)
•fortunate

Ashley (Anglo-Saxon)
•of the ash tree meadow

Atlas (Greek)
•lifted, carried

Aubrey (Teutonic)
•ruler of the elves

Auburn (Uncertain)
•fine-appearing

August (Latin)
•venerable, majestic

Austin (Latin)
•useful

Axel (Hebrew)
•man of peace

Aziz (Arabic)
•strong

B

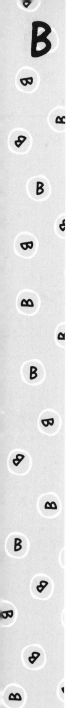

Bailey (Old French)
•Bailiff or steward

Bain (Irish)
•fair bridge

Baird (Celtic)
•bard or minstrel

Baker (English)
•baker

Baldwin (Teutonic)
•friendly, bold

Ballard (German)
•brave, strong

Bancroft (Anglo-Saxon)
•from the bean field

Banning (Irish)
•small and fair

Barclay (Scottish, English)
•birch tree meadow

Barden (Old English)
•barley valley

Barker (English)
•lumberjack, advertiser at a carnival

Barlow (Old English)
•dweller on the bare hill

Barnabas (Hebrew, Greek)
•son of consolation

Barnes (English)
•bear

Barnett (English)
•nobleman, leader

Barnum (German, English)
•barn, storage, baron's home

Baron (German, English)
•nobleman, baron

Barrett (Teutonic)
•bear-like

Barry (Celtic, Irish, French)
•straight-forward, spear, marksman, gate, fence

Bartholomew (Hebrew)
•warlike son

Barton (English)
•barley farm

Basil (Greek, Latin)
•royal

Baxter (Old English)
•baker

Beacher (English)
•beech trees

Beau (French)
•handsome

Beaufort (French)
•beautiful fort

Beaumont (French)
•beautiful mountain

Beck (English, Scandinavian)
•brook

Bela (Czech, Hungarian)
•white, bright

Bell (French, English)
•handsome, bell ringer

Benedict (Latin)
•blessed

Benjamin (Anglo-Saxon)
•of the moors

Bentley (English)
•moor, coarse grass meadow

Berk (Turkish)
•solid, rugged

Berkeley (Anglo-Saxon)
•from the birch meadow

Bernard (Teutonic)
•bold as a bear

Berry (English)
•berry, grape

Bert (Teutonic, English)
•bright

Bertram (English, German)
•bright raven, illustrious

Berwyn (English)
•harvest son, powerful friend

Bevan (Celtic)
•son of Evan

Beverley (Anglo-Saxon)
•from the beaver meadow

Bevis (French)
•bull

Bijan (Persian)
•ancient hero

Birch (English)
•white, shining, birch tree

Birney (English)
•island with a brook

Bishop (Greek, English)
•overseer, bishop

Bjorn (Scandinavian)
•bear

Blackburn (Scottish)
•black brook

Blade (English)
•knife, sword

Blaine (Celtic, English)
•thin or lean, river source

Blair (Celtic, Irish)
•a place, plain, field

Blake (Old English)
•pale, shining, attractive, dark

Blanco (Spanish)
•light skinned, white, blond

Blaze (Latin, English)
•stammerer, flame, trail

Bliss (English)
•blissful, joyful

Bly (Native American)
•high

Bogart (German, Irish, Welsh)
•strong as a bow, bog, marshland

Bond (English)
•tiller of the soil

Boniface (Latin)
•do-gooder

Booker (English)
•bookmaker, book lover, Bible lover

Boone (Latin, French)
•good

Booth (Teutonic, English)
•home lover, hut, temporary dwelling

Borden (Old English, French)
•he lives near the boar's den, cottage

Borg (Scandinavian)
•castle

Boris (Slavonic)
•warrior

B

Bosley (English)
•grove of trees

Bowen (Celtic)
•son of Owen

Boyd (Celtic)
•yellow-haired

Bradford (Anglo-Saxon)
•from the broad ford, broad river crossing

Bradley (Anglo-Saxon)
•from the broad meadow

Bradshaw (English)
•broad forest

Brady (Irish, Old English)
•spirited, broad eye, broad island

Brainard (English)
•bold raven, prince

Bram (Scottish)
•bramble, brushwood

Brand (English)
•a fighter, firebrand, sword

Brandon (English)
•hill covered with broom, beacon hill

Brandy (Dutch)
•brandy

Breck (Irish)
•freckled

Brenden (Irish, English)
•prince, little raven, sword

Brennan (Irish)
•drop of water, tear

Brent (Old English)
•from the steep hill

Brett (Celtic)
•from Great Britain

Brewster (English)
•brewer

Brian (Celtic)
•strong, sincere

Brice (Celtic)
•ambitious

Brick (English)
•bridge

Brigham (Old English, French)
•dweller by the bridge, troops, brigade

Bromley (Old English)
•dweller in the meadow

Brock (Celtic)
•badger

Broderick (Welsh, English)
•son of the famous ruler, broad ridge

Brody (Scottish, Irish)
•muddy place, ditch, canal builder

Brook (English)
•brook, stream

Brown (English)
•brown, bear

Bruce (French, Gaelic)
•brushwood thicket, woods, positive, daring

Bruno (Teutonic)
•brown haired, brown skinned

Bevan (Celtic)
•son of Evan

Buckley (English)
•deer meadow

Buckminster (English)
•preacher

Bud (English)
•herald, messenger

Burgess (Teutonic, English)
•a townsman, shopkeeper

Burke (Teutonic)
•from the castle

Burr (Swedish, English)
•youth, prickly plant

Burton (Anglo-Saxon)
•of bright fame, fortified town

Buster (American)
•hitter, puncher

Byram (English)
•cattleyard

Byrd (English)
•birdlike

Byron (French, English)
•from the cottage, barn

Cade (Old English)
•lump, pet

Cadman (Celtic)
•brave warrior

Cadmus (Greek)
•from the east

Caesar (Latin)
•purposeful, long haired

Cahil (Turkish)
•young, naive

Cain (Hebrew)
•spear, gatherer

Cairn (Welsh)
•landmark of piled-up stones

Cairo (Arabic)
•capital of Egypt

Calder (Celtic)
•from the river of stones

Caldwell (English)
•cold well

Caleb (Hebrew, Arabic)
•a dog lover, faithful, bold, brave

Calhoun (Irish, Scottish)
•narrow woods, warrior

Callahan (Irish)
•a Catholic saint

Calvert (Old English)
•herdsman

Calvin (Latin)
•bald, bold

Camden (Scottish)
•winding valley

Cameron (Celtic, Scottish)
•crooked nose

Camilo (Latin)
•child born to freedom, noble

Campbell (French, Scottish)
•from a bright field, beautiful field, crooked mouth

Candide (Latin)
•pure, sincere

Cannon (French)
•church official, large gun

Carey (Greek, Welsh)
•pure, castle, rocky island

Carl (Teutonic, German, English)
•forceful, farmer, strong

Carlin (Irish)
•little champion

C

Carlyle (Old English)
•from the walled city

Carmel (Hebrew)
•vineyard, garden

Carmen (Latin)
•song

Carmine (Latin)
•song, crimson

Carney (Irish, Scottish)
•victorious, fighter

Carr (Scandinavian)
•marsh

Carrol (Celtic)
•champion

Carson (Welsh)
•his father lives near
marshes

Carter (Old English)
•cart-driver

Carver (Anglo-Saxon)
•carver, sculptor

Cartwright (English)
•cart builder

Cary (Celtic)
•from the fortress

Casey (Celtic)
•valorous

Cash (Latin)
•vain

Caspar (Persian, German)
•gift-bearer, treasurer,
imperial

Cassidy (Irish)
•clever, curly haired

Cassius (Latin, French)
•box, protective cover

Castle (Latin)
•castle

Castor (Greek)
•beaver

Cato (Latin)
•knowledgeable, wise

Cecil (Latin)
•harmony, blind

Cedric (Celtic, English)
•chieftain

Chadwick (Old English)
•from the warrior's town,
defender

Chaim (Hebrew)
•life

Chalmers (Scottish)
•private servant, son of the lo

Chan (Sanskrit)
•shining

Chanan (Hebrew)
•cloud

Chancellor (English)
•record keeper

Chander (Hindi)
•moon

Chandler (French)
•candle maker

Chaney (French)
•oak

Channing (Anglo-Saxon)
•knowing, canon, church
official

Chapin (French)
•man of gold

Chapman (English)
•merchant

Charles (Teutonic)
•manly, man of the people, farmer

Charro (Spanish)
•cowboy

Chase (Old French)
•hunter

Chauncey (French, English)
•official, chancellor

Cherokee (Native American)
•people of a different speech

Chester (Old English)
•dweller in a fortified town

Cheung (Chinese)
•good luck

Chico (Spanish)
•boy

Chiko (Japanese)
•arrow, pledge

Christian (Latin, Greek)
•follower of Christ, anointed

Christopher (Greek)
•Christ-bearer

Churchhill (English)
•church on the hill

Cian (Irish)
•ancient

Cicero (Latin)
•chickpea

Clancy (Irish)
•red-headed fighter

Clarence (Latin)
•bright

Clark (Latin, French)
•wise, cleric, scholar

Claude (Latin, French)
•affectionate, lame

Clayton (Teutonic, English)
•from the town on the clay bed

Clement (Latin)
•merciful

Cletus (Greek)
•illustrious

Cleveland (English)
•land of cliffs, hilly district

Clifford (Saxon)
•valorous

Clifton (Old English)
•from the farm at the cliff

Clinton (Teutonic)
•from the headland farm

Clovis (German)
•famous soldier

Clyde (Welsh, Scottish)
•heard from afar, warm

Cochise (Native American)
•famous Apache warrior and chief

Cody (Irish, English)
•son of Odo, cushion

Colbert (English)
•famous seafarer

Colby (Old English)
•from the black farm, dark

Cole (Latin)
•cabbage farmer

Coleman (Celtic, English)
•dove, coal miner

Colin (Celtic, Irish)
•strong, young and virile, young cub

C

Collier (English)
•miner

Colson (Greek, English)
•son of Nicholas

Colt (English)
•young horse, frisky

Columbus (Greek, Latin)
•curious, dove

Conan (Celtic, Irish, Scottish)
•high and mighty, praised

Conlan (Irish)
•hero

Connor (Irish, Scottish)
•wolf-lover, wise

Conrad (Teutonic)
•bold counsel, resolute

Conroy (Celtic)
•wise

Constantine (Latin)
•unwavering

Conway (Celtic)
•man of the great plains

Coolidge (Uncertain)
•careful and protective

Cooper (Middle English)
•maker of barrels, vats, buckets

Corbin (Latin)
•the raven

Corcoran (Irish)
•ruddy

Cordell (French)
•rope maker

Cordero (Spanish)
•little lamb

Corey (Irish)
•hollow

Cormac (Irish)
•raven's son

Cornelius (Latin, Greek)
•studious, noble, cornel tree

Cortez (Spanish)
•dweller at a royal court, conqueror

Corwin (English)
•heart's companion

Cosmo (Greek)
•orderly, harmonious, universe

Coty (French)
•old house, slope, hillside

Cowan (Irish)
•hillside hollow

Coyle (Irish)
•leader in battle

Coyne (French)
•modest

Craig (Saxon, Irish, Scottish)
•crag dweller

Crawford (Old English)
•of the crow's ford

Creed (Latin)
•belief

Cromwell (English)
•crooked spring, winding spring

Crosby (Scandinavian)
•dweller by the town cross

Crosley (English)
•meadow of the cross

Cruz (Portuguese, Spanish)
•cross

Cullen (Irish)
•woods

Curran (Irish)
•hero

Curtis (Old French, Latin)
•courteous, enclosure

Cuthbert (English)
•brilliant

Cutler (English)
•knife maker

Cyrano (Greek)
•from the Cyrene

Cyril (Greek)
•lordly

Cyrus (Persian)
•throne, sun

Dakota (Native American)
•tribal name, friend, partner

Dale (Teutonic, Old English)
•dweller in the dale, valley, hollow

Dalton (Old English)
•from the farm in the dale

Damian (Greek)
•tame, soother

Damon (Greek, Latin)
•constant, loyal, spirit

Dana (Scandinavian)
•a Dane

Dane (Old English, French)
•valley, honorable

Daniel (Hebrew)
•God has judged

Dante (Latin)
•lasting, enduring

Daren (Hausa)
•born at night

Darius (Persian, Greek)
•dark, strong, he who upholds good, wealthy

Darnell (Middle English)
•hidden nook

Darren (Irish, English)
•black oak, great, rocky hill

Daryl (Old English, French)
•beloved, dear

David (Hebrew)
•beloved

Davin (Scandinavian)
•bright man

Davis (Welsh)
•son of David

Dayton (English)
•day town, bright, sunny town

Deacon (Greek)
•one who serves

Dean (Old English, Latin)
•from the valley, chief of ten, church official

Dedrick (German)
•ruler of the people

Delaney (Irish)
•descendent of the challenger

Delbert (Teutonic, English)
•bright and noble

D

Delmar (Latin)
•of the sea

Delroy (French)
•belonging to the king

Delsin (Native American)
•he is so

Delvin (Irish, English)
•fierce courage, friend

Demetrius (Greek)
•lover of the earth

Dempsey (Irish)
•proud

Dennis (Greek)
•worshiper

Denton (English)
•happy home

Derek (Teutonic)
•ruler of the people

Dermot (Irish, English)
•free from envy, free

Deron (Hebrew)
•bird, freedom

Derren (Irish)
•great

Desmond (Celtic)
•sophistic

Destin (French)
•destiny, fate

Devin (Irish, Old French)
•poet, fawn, excellent

Devlin (Irish)
•brave, fierce

Dewey (Welsh)
•prized, controlled physical power

DeWitt (Flemish)
•blond

Dexter (Latin, Old English)
•adroit, fortunate, dyer

Dieter (German)
•army of the people

Dillon (Celtic)
•faithful and true

Dino (German)
•little sword

Dolan (Irish)
•dark haired

Domingo (Spanish)
•born on Sunday

Dominic (Latin)
•belong to the Lord

Don (Celtic, Latin)
•dark or brown

Donahue (Irish)
•dark warrior

Donald (Celtic)
•world ruler

Donato (Italian)
•gift

Donovan (Irish)
•dark brown swarthy person

Doran (Greek, Hebrew, Irish)
•gift, stranger, exile

Dorian (Greek)
•from Doris

Dougal (Scottish)
•dark stranger

Douglas (Celtic, Scottish)
•thoughtful, dark blue, dark water

Doyle (Celtic)
•dark stranger

Drake (Old English)
•dragon, male duck

Drew (Teutonic, Greek)
•honest, to carry, manly

Driscoll (Celtic)
•the interpreter

Drummond (Scottish)
•druid's mountain

Dryden (English)
•dry valley

Dugan (Irish)
•dark

Duncan (Celtic)
•brown chief

Dunlop (Scottish)
•muddy hill

Durand (Latin)
•lasting friend

Dustin (English, Old German)
•dusty place, brave warrior

Dwayne (Celtic, Irish)
•singing, black, swarthy

Dwight (Teutonic)
•white, fair

Dylan (Welsh)
•of the sea, son of the waves

Eagan (Irish)
•very mighty

Earl (Old English, Irish)
•noble warrior, pledge

Eaton (Anglo-Saxon)
•of the river

Ebenezer (Hebrew)
•stone of help, foundation stone

Edan (Celtic)
•flame

Eden (Hebrew)
•delightful

Edgar (Old English)
•wealth, spear

Edmund (Old English)
•protector of wealth

Edward (Old English)
•guardian of wealth

Elden (Teutonic)
•respected

Elijah (Hebrew)
•faithful to God

Elliott (Hebrew)
•faithful to God

Ellsworth (Anglo-Saxon)
•lover of the earth

Elmer (Anglo-Saxon)
•excellent, famous

Elmo (Greek)
•lovable, friendly

Elmore (English)
•moor where the elm trees grow

Elroy (Latin)
•royal

Elton (Anglo-Saxon)
•from the old farm

Elvis (Irish, Scandinavian)
•white, wise

F

Elwood (Anglo-Saxon)
•friend of the elves

Emilio (Spanish, Latin)
•rival

Emmanuel (Hebrew)
•God is with us

Emerson (Teutonic)
•son of Emery

Emery (Teutonic)
•dutiful, industrious leader

Emil (Teutonic, Latin)
•industrious, flatterer

Emmett (Anglo-Saxon, German)
•diligence, energetic

Engelbert (German)
•bright as an angel

Ennis (Greek)
•mine

Ephraim (Hebrew)
•very fruitful

Erasmus (Greek)
•amiable

Ercole (Italian)
•splendid gift

Eric (Teutonic, Scandinavian)
•princely, ruler

Erin (Irish)
•peaceful

Ernest (Greek, German)
•serious, vigor, earnestness

Errol (Teutonic, Latin)
•a nobleman, wanderer

Ervin (English)
•sea friend

Este (Italian)
•east

Ethan (Hebrew)
•strength, steadfast

Euclid (Greek)
•intelligent

Eugene (Greek)
•well-born

Eustace (Greek, Latin)
•productive, stable, calm

Evan (English, Irish)
•challenger, young warrior

Evelyn (Old English)
•a dear youth, hazelnut

Everett (Teutonic)
•mighty as a boar

Ezekiel (Hebrew)
•God's strength

Ezra (Hebrew)
•dawn, beginning of joy, help

Fabian (Latin)
•prosperous farmer

Fagan (Irish)
•little fiery one

Fairbanks (Uncertain)
•sympathetic

Fairfax (Anglo-Saxon)
•fair-haired

Farley (Old English)
•meadow of the sheep

Farr (English)
•traveler

Farrell (Celtic)
•man of valor

Faust (Latin)
•lucky, fortunate

Favian (Latin)
•man of understanding

Felix (Latin)
•fortunate, happy

Ferdinand (Teutonic)
•adventurous

Fergus (Celtic)
•strong man

Ferris (Celtic)
•rock

Fidel (Latin)
•faithful

Fielding (English)
•field, field worker

Filbert (English)
•brilliant

Finian (Irish)
•light-skinned, white

Finn (German, Irish, Norwegian)
•from Finland, light-
skinned, from the Lapland

Fiorello (Italian)
•little flower

Firman (Anglo-Saxon, French)
•traveler to far places,
firm, strong

Fitzgerald (English)
•son of Gerald

Fitzpatrick (English)
•son of Patrick

Flavian (Latin)
•blond, fair-haired

Fletcher (French, English)
•arrow maker

Flint (English)
•stream, flintstone

Florian (Latin)
•flowering, blooming

Floyd (Celtic, Irish)
•the gray, will of God

Flynn (Irish)
•son of the red-haired man

Fontaine (French)
•fountain

Forbes (Irish)
•prosperous

Forrest (Teutonic)
•from the woods

Fortune (French)
•fortunate, lucky

Foster (Teutonic)
•keeper of the woods

Fowler (English)
•trapper of wild fowl

Francis (Latin)
•Frenchman; free

Franklin (Teutonic, English)
•free man

Fraser (French, English)
•strawberry, curly haired

Frederick (Teutonic)
•peaceful ruler

Freeman (Anglo-Saxon)
•one born free

Fremont (German)
•free, noble protector

Fulbright (German)
•very bright

Fuller (English)
•cloth thickener

G

Gabriel (Hebrew)
•man of God

Gage (Old French)
•fixed measure, pledge

Galbraith (Irish)
•Scotsman in Ireland

Gallagher (Irish)
•eager helper

Galvin (Celtic)
•the sparrow

Galway (Irish, Celtic)
•strange

Gannon (Irish)
•fair-skinned

Garcia (Spanish)
•mighty with a spear

Gardner (Middle English)
•gardener

Gareth (Welsh)
•gentle

Garfield (English)
•field of spears, battlefield

Garland (Old French)
•crowned for victory

Garnet (Latin)
•red jewel, pomegranate seed

Garrett (Irish)
•brave spearman

Garrison (French)
•troops stationed at a ford

Garth (Scandinavian, English)
•yard-keeper, enclosure, garden

Garvin (Teutonic)
•friend

Gary (German)
•mighty spearman

Gavin (Teutonic, Welsh)
•battle hawk

Gaylord (Anglo-Saxon, French)
•joyous noble, lively, high-spirited

Gaynor (Irish)
•son of the fair-skinned man

Geoffrey (Teutonic)
•God's peace, brave

George (Greek)
•farmer

Gerald (Teutonic)
•dominion with the spear

Germaine (French, English)
•from Germany, sprout, bud

Gideon (Hebrew)
•the deliverer, tree cutter

Gifford (Teutonic, English)
•gift, bold giver

Gil (Greek, Hebrew)
•shield bearer, happy

Gilbert (Teutonic)
•bright pledge, progressive

Giles (Latin, Greek, French)
•shield bearer, kid, goatskin shield

Gillespie (Irish)
•son of the bishop's servant

Gilmore (Irish)
•devoted to the Virgin Mary

Gilroy (Latin)
•king's servant

Glen (Celtic, Irish)
•from the valley or glen

Godfrey (Teutonic, Irish)
•quiet, God's peace

Godwin (English)
•friend of God

Goliath (Hebrew)
•exiled

Gomer (Hebrew, English)
•completed, finished, famous battle

Gordon (Scottish, English)
•generous, triangular hill

Grady (Irish)
•noble, illustrious

Graham (Scottish, English)
•from the gray home, grand home

Grant (Latin, French)
•great, grand, tall

Gray (English)
•gray haired

Gregory (Greek, Latin)
•vigilant

Griffin (Latin)
•hooked nose

Griffith (Latin, Welsh)
•having great faith, fierce chief, ruddy

Grover (Anglo-Saxon)
•grove-dweller

Gunther (Scandinavian)
•bold warrior

Gustave (Scandinavian)
•noble staff

Guthrie (Celtic, Irish)
•war serpent, windy spot

Guy (French, German, Hebrew)
•leader, guide, wood, wide, valley

Hackett (German, French)
•little woodcutter

Hagen (Irish)
•young, youthful

Hakeem (Arabic)
•most wise

Haley (Irish)
•ingenious

Hali (Greek)
•sea

Hall (Old English)
•from the master's house

Hamal (Arabic)
•lamb

Hamilton (French, English)
•from the beautiful mountain, proud estate

Hamlet (German, French)
•little village, home

Hammet (English, Scandinavian)
•village

Harcourt (French)
•from the armed court

Harden (English)
•valley of the hares

Harding (English)
•brave man's son

Hardwin (English)
•brave friend

H

Hargrove (English)
•grove of the hares

Harlan (Teutonic, Old English)
•from the land of warriors, gray land

Harley (Anglo-Saxon)
•from the hare's meadow

Harold (Anglo-Saxon)
•commander of the army

Harper (Old English)
•harp player

Harrison (Old English)
•noble

Hartman (German)
•hard, strong

Hartwell (English)
•deer hill

Harvey (Celtic, French, German)
•bitter, strong, ardent, army warrior

Hasad (Turkish)
•reaper, harvester

Hashim (Arabic)
•crusher of evil

Hasin (Hindi)
•laughing

Hastings (Latin, English)
•spear, house council

Haven (Dutch, English)
•harbor, port, safe place

Hawthorne (English)
•hawthorn tree

Hayden (English, Irish)
•from the hedged hill, hay valley, armor

Hayes (Old English)
•from the woods

Haywood (English)
•hedged forest

Heathcliff (English)
•cliff near the heath

Heaton (English)
•high place

Hector (Greek)
•unswerving, steadfast

Hedley (English)
•heather-filled meadow

Helmer (German)
•warrior's wrath

Helmut (Greek, German)
•helmet of courage

Heman (Hebrew)
•faithful

Henderson (Scottish, English)
•son of Henry

Henry (Teutonic)
•ruler of the home

Herbert (Teutonic)
•illustrious warrior

Hercules (Greek)
•glorious gift

Herman (Teutonic, Latin)
•warrior, noble

Hermes (Greek)
•messenger

Herrod (Hebrew)
•heroic conqueror

Hershel (Hebrew)
•deer

Hertz (Yiddish)
•my strife

Hewitt (German, French)
•little smart one

Heywood (Teutonic, English)
•from the dark green forest

Hilary (Latin)
•cheerful, merry

Hildebrand (German)
•battle sword

Hilel (Arabic)
•new moon

Hilton (English)
•town on a hill

Hippolyte (Greek)
•horseman

Hiram (Hebrew)
•noble born, exalted

Hobart (German)
•Bart's hill

Hogan (Irish)
•youth

Holbrook (Anglo-Saxon)
•from the valley brook

Holden (Teutonic, Old English)
•kind, deep valley

Hollis (Anglo-Saxon)
•dweller by the holly trees

Holmes (English)
•river islands

Holt (English)
•forest

Homer (Greek)
•pledge, secure

Honesto (Filipino)
•honest

Honorato (Spanish)
•honorable

Hop (Chinese)
•agreeable

Horace (Latin)
•worthy to be beheld

Horatio (Latin)
•clan name

Horst (German)
•dense grove, thicket

Horton (English)
•garden estate

Houston (English, Scottish)
•Hugh's town, hill town

Howard (Teutonic)
•chief guardian

Howell (Welsh)
•remarkable

Howland (English)
•hilly land

Hoyt (Irish)
•spirit, mind

Hu (Chinese)
•tiger

Hubert (Teutonic)
•bright in spirit

Hume (Teutonic)
•lover of his home

Humphrey (Teutonic)
•protector of the peace

Hung (Vietnamese)
•brave

Hunter (Middle English)
•huntsman

Hurley (Irish)
•sea tide

Hussein (Arabic)
•small handsome one

Hutchinson (English)
•son of the hutch dweller

H

Hyatt (English)
•high gate

Hyde (English)
•measure of land equal to 120 acres

Hyman (Hebrew)
•life

Ichabod (Hebrew)
•the glory has departed

Ignatius (Latin)
•fiery and ardent

Igor (Scandinavian)
•hero

Ilan (Hebrew, Basque)
•tree, youth

Ingram (Teutonic, English)
•the raven, angel

Ira (Hebrew)
•watchful

Irving (Irish, Welsh, English)
•handsome, white river, sea friend

Isaac (Hebrew)
•mirthful; glad

Ishmael (Hebrew)
•God will hear

Isidore (Greek)
•gift

Jacinto (Portuguese, Spanish)
•hyacinth

Jackson (Old English)
•son of Jack

Jacob (Hebrew)
•supplanter, substitute

Jade (Spanish)
•jade, precious stone

Jaegar (German)
•hunter

Jakeem (Arabic)
•uplifted

Jamal (Arabic)
•handsomeness

James (Hebrew)
•the supplanter

Janus (Latin)
•gate, passageway, born in Januar

Jared (Hebrew, Akkadian)
•descendent, servant

Jarek (Slavonic)
•born in January

Jarvis (Teutonic)
•sharp as a spear

Jason (Greek)
•healer

Jasper (Persian)
•bringer of treasure

Javier (Spanish)
•owner of a new house

Jay (Anglo-Saxon, Old French)
•crow, or lively, bluejay

Jed (Arabic)
•hand

Jedrek (Polish)
•strong, manly

Jefferson (Old English)
•son of Jeffrey

Jenkin (Flemish)
•little John

Jeremiah (Hebrew)
•exalted by the Lord

Jericho (Arabic)
•city of the moon

Jermaine (Latin, English)
•from Germany, sprout, bud

Jerome (Greek, Latin)
•having a holy name, exalted

Jerry (German)
•mighty spearman

Jesse (Hebrew)
•God's grace, God exists, wealthy

Jesus (Greek)
•God saves

Jethro (Hebrew)
•outstanding, abundant

Jin (Chinese)
•gold

Joachim (Hebrew)
•the Lord will judge

Job (Hebrew)
•the afflicted

Joel (Hebrew)
•Jehovah is God

John (Hebrew)
•God is gracious, given by God

Jonas (Hebrew)
•dove, he accomplishes

Jordan (Hebrew)
•descending

Joseph (Hebrew)
•he shall add

Josha (Hindi)
•satisfied

Joshi (Swahili)
•galloping

Joshua (Hebrew)
•Jehovah saves

Josiah (Hebrew)
•he is healed by the Lord

Jovan (Latin)
•love-like, majestic

Jubal (Hebrew)
•ram's horn

Judah (Hebrew)
•praised

Judson (Middle English)
•son of Judd

Julian (Latin)
•kind, downy hair

Julias (Roman)
•descended from Jove, clan name

Julius (Greek, Latin)
•youthful, downy-bearded

Junior (Latin)
•young

Juro (Japanese)
•best wishes, long life

Jurrien (Dutch)
•God will uplift

Justin (Latin)
•just

J

K

Kadar (Arabic)
•powerful

Kadeem (Arabic)
•servant, ancient

Kala (Hindi, Hawaiian)
•black, time, sun

Kalama (Hawaiian)
•torch

Kamal (Hindi, Arabic)
•lotus, perfect

Kane (Celtic, Japanese)
•radiant, warrior, golden, eastern sky

Kantu (Hindi)
•happy

Kanu (Swahili)
•wildcat

Kareem (Arabic)
•noble

Karif (Arabic)
•born in autumn

Karsten (Greek)
•anointed

Kaseem (Arabic)
•divided

Kasen (Basque)
•protected with a helmet

Kasimir (Arabic)
•peace

Kasper (Persian)
•treasure

Kass (German)
•blackbird

Kato (Runyankore)
•second of twins

Kavan (Irish)
•handsome

Kavi (Hindi)
•poet

Kay (English, Greek, German)
•strong, determined

Keane (English, German, Irish)
•sharp, tall, handsome

Keaton (English)
•where hawks fly

Keb (Egyptian)
•earth

Keefe (Irish)
•handsome, loved

Keegan (Irish)
•fire

Keenan (Irish)
•enduring, small and ancient

Keene (German, English)
•bold, smart

Keiji (Japanese)
•cautious ruler

Keir (Scottish)
•swarthy

Keitaro (Japanese)
•blessed

Keith (Welsh, Scottish)
•wood-dweller

Kelby (Teutonic)
•from the farm by the spring

Kele (Native American-Hopi)
•sparrow hawk

Kell *(Scandinavian)*
•spring

Kellen *(German, Irish)*
•swamp, mighty warrior

Keller *(Irish)*
•little companion

Kelly *(Irish)*
•impetuous, gentle & helpful

Kelsey *(Scandinavian)*
•dweller by the water,
island of ships

Kendall *(Celtic)*
•chief of the valley

Kendrick *(Welsh, Scottish)*
•royal ruler

Kennedy *(Irish)*
•helmeted chief

Kenneth *(Celtic, English)*
•handsome, fire-sprung,
royal oath

Kent *(Celtic)*
•white or bright, coast

Kentaro *(Japanese)*
•big boy

Kentrell *(English)*
•king's estate

Kenyon *(Celtic)*
•fair-haired

Kenzie *(Scottish)*
•wise leader

Kerey *(Gypsy)*
•homeward-bound

Kermit *(Celtic)*
•free

Kerr *(Celtic)*
•dark, mysterious

Kevin *(Celtic, Irish)*
•kind, gentle, loved,
beautiful birth, handsome

Key *(English)*
•key, protected

Khan *(Turkish)*
•prince

Khiry *(Arabic)*
•benevolent

Khoury *(Arabic)*
•priest

Kibo *(Uset)*
•worldly, wise

Kidd *(English)*
•child, young goat

Kieran *(Irish)*
•little and dark

Kincaid *(Scottish)*
•battle chief

Kipp *(English)*
•pointed hill

Kirby *(Teutonic, English)*
•from the church village,
cottage by the water

Kirk *(Scandinavian, Scottish)*
•living close to the church

Kito *(Swahili)*
•jewel, precious child

Kiyoshi *(Japanese)*
•quiet, peaceful

Knowles *(English)*
•grassy slope

Knox *(English)*
•hill

Knute *(Danish)*
•kind

L

Kofi (Twi)
•born on Friday

Kojo (Akan)
•born on Monday

Kosey (African)
•lion

Krishna (Hindi)
•delightful, pleasurable

Kumar (Sanskrit)
•prince

Kwame (Akan)
•born on a Saturday

Kwan (Korean)
•strong

Kyle (Scottish, Irish)
•fair, handsome, narrow piece of land

Kyler (Dutch)
•archer, wild boar

Kynan (Welsh)
•chief

Kyros (Greek)
•master

Ladd (English)
•attendant

Laird (Celtic)
•proprietor

Lamar (English, German, French)
•cooperative, land famous, sea, ocean

Lambert (Teutonic)
•rich in land

Lamont (Scandinavian, French)
•lawyer, the mountain

Lance (Anglo-Saxon, French)
•spear, servant

Landon (Anglo-Saxon)
•from the long hill

Landry (French, English)
•ruler of the place

Lane (Anglo-Saxon)
•from the country road

Lang (Scandinavian, Teutonic)
•tall man

Langdon (English)
•the long hill

Lanford (Old English)
•long ford

Langley (English)
•the long meadow

Langston (English)
•narrow, long town

Laramie (French)
•tears of love

Larkin (Irish)
•rough, fierce

LaSalle (French)
•hill

Laszlo (Hungarian)
•famous ruler

Latham (Scandinavian, English)
•barn, district

Lathrop (Anglo-Saxon)
•of the village, farmstead

Lawrence (Latin)
•victorious, crowned with laurels

Leander (Greek)
•brave, like a lion

Lear (Teutonic)
•of the meadow

Lee (Anglo-Saxon)
•sheltered; meadow

Leland (Old English)
•from the meadow land

Len (Native American-Hopi)
•flute

Leo (Latin)
•lion

Leonard (Teutonic)
•brave or strong as a lion

Leopold (Teutonic)
•patriotic, brave people

Leroy (French)
•royal, king

Leslie (Celtic, Scottish)
•from the gray fort, garden by the pool

Lester (Anglo-Saxon, Latin)
•from the army or camp

Lev (Hebrew)
•heart

Levi (Hebrew)
•a bond or promise, joined, attached

Lewin (English)
•beloved friend

Lewis (Teutonic)
•famous warrior

Lincoln (Celtic)
•from the place by the pool

Linus (Hebrew, Greek)
•flax-haired

Lionel (Old French)
•a young lion

Litton (English)
•town on the hill

Lloyd (Celtic, Welsh)
•gray, holy

Lobo (Spanish)
•wolf

Locke (English)
•forest

Logan (Scottish, Irish)
•little hollow, meadow

London (English)
•fortress of the moon

Long (Chinese, Vietnamese)
•dragon, hair

Lorcan (Irish)
•little, fierce

Lorimer (Latin)
•lover of horses, harness maker

Loring (Teutonic)
•from Lorraine, son of the famous warrior

Loris (Dutch)
•clown

Lot (Hebrew)
•veiled

Loudon (German)
•low valley

Louis (German)
•famous warrior

Lourdes (French)
•from Lourdes, France

Lowell (Anglo-Saxon, French)
•beloved, wolf cub

Lucius (Latin)
•light

M

Lucas (Latin)
•man from Lucania

Ludlow (English)
•prince's hill

Luke (Latin)
•light

Lundy (Scottish)
•grove by the island

Lunn (Irish)
•warlike

Luther (Teutonic)
•renowned warrior

Lyle (French)
•from the island

Lyndon (Old English)
•of the linden tree, hill
with lime trees

Lynn (Anglo-Saxon)
•from the waterfalls, brook

Lysander (Greek)
•liberator

Mac (Scottish)
•son

Macadam (Scottish)
•son of Adam

Macallister (Irish)
•son of Alistair

Macario (Spanish)
•happy, blessed

Macarthur (Irish)
•son of Arthur

Macaulay (Scottish)
•son of righteousness

Macbride (Scottish)
•son of a follower of Saint
Brigid

Maccoy (Irish)
•son of Hugh

Maccrea (Irish)
•son of grace

Macdonald (Scottish)
•son of Donald

Macdougal (Scottish)
•son of Dougal

Mackenzie (Scottish)
•son of Kenneth

Mackinley (Irish)
•son of the learned ruler

Macon (German, English)
•maker

Macy (French)
•enduring material, Matthew's
estate

Madison (Teutonic, English)
•mighty in battle

Magee (Irish)
•son of Hugh

Mahir (Arabic, Hebrew)
•excellent, industrious

Mahon (Irish)
•bear

Malachi (Hebrew)
•angel of God

Malcolm (Irish, Scottish)
•servant of St. Columbus, dove

Malden (English)
•meeting place in a pasture

Malik (Arabic, Punjabi)
•king, lord, master

Malin (English)
•strong, little warrior

Mallory (English, French)
•luckless, army counselor, wild duck

Mandel (German)
•almond

Manford (English)
•small ford

Manfred (Teutonic)
•peace among men

Manheim (German)
•servant's home

Manley (English)
•hero's meadow

Mannix (Irish)
•monk

Mansfield (English)
•field by the river

Manzo (Japanese)
•third son

Marcus (Latin)
•warlike

Marid (Arabic)
•rebellious

Marin (French)
•sailor

Marion (Welsh, French)
•sea hill, bitter

Mark (Latin)
•martial, defender

Markham (English)
•homestead on the boundary

Marland (English)
•lake land

Marlin (English)
•deep-sea fish

Marlow (English)
•hill by the lake

Marmaduke (Celtic)
•sea leader

Mars (Latin)
•bold warrior

Marsden (Anglo-Saxon)
•from the marsh valley

Marshall (Old French)
•marshal, horse groom, leader of men

Marston (English)
•town by the marsh

Martell (English)
•hammerer

Martin (Latin)
•unyielding, of Mars

Marvin (Teutonic)
•famous friend or sea friend

Masaccio (Italian)
•twin

Masata (Japanese)
•just

Maslin (French)
•little Thomas

Mason (Latin, French)
•stone worker

Massey (English)
•twin

Matalino (Filipino)
•bright

Mather (English)
•powerful army

M

M

Matson (Hebrew)
•son of Matt

Matthew (Hebrew)
•gift of God

Maurice (Latin)
•moorish, dark

Maverick (American)
•independent

Maxfield (English)
•Mack's field

Maxime (French)
•most excellent

Maximilian (Latin)
•the greatest

Maxwell (Anglo-Saxon)
•dweller by the spring

Maynard (Anglo-Saxon)
•mightily brave

Mckay (Scottish)
•son of Kay

Mead (English)
•meadow

Medwin (German)
•faithful friend

Meinhard (German)
•strong, firm

Meinrad (German)
•strong counsel

Meir (Hebrew)
•one who brightens, shines

Meka (Hawaiian)
•eyes

Melchior (Hebrew)
•king

Melvern (Native American)
•great chief

Melvin (Irish, English)
•gentle chief, council

Mendel (English)
•repairman

Mercer (English)
•storekeeper

Meredith (Celtic)
•protector from the sea

Merle (French)
•blackbird

Merlin (Celtic)
•falcon, hawk

Merrill (Teutonic, French, Irish)
•famous, bright sea

Merritt (Latin, Irish)
•valuable, deserving

Merton (Anglo-Saxon)
•from the place by the sea

Meyer (Teutonic)
•farmer

Micah (Hebrew)
•like unto the Lord

Michael (Hebrew)
•who is like God?

Michio (Japanese)
•man with the strength of three thousand

Milburn (Old English)
•from the millstream

Miles (Slavonic, German, Greek)
•soldier, merciful, generous, millstone

Miller (English)
•grain grinder

Milos (Greek, Slavonic)
•pleasant

Milton (Anglo-Saxon)
•from the mill town

Mohammad (Arabic)
•praiseworthy

Mohan (Hindi)
•delightful

Monroe (Irish)
•man from Roe

Montague (Latin, Spanish)
•from the peaked mountain

Montaro (Japanese)
•big boy

Montez (Spanish)
•dweller in the mountains

Montgomery (French)
•mountain hunter

Montreal (French)
•royal mountain

Moore (French)
•dark, moor, marshland

Mordecai (Hebrew)
•wise counselor

Morell (French)
•dark, from Morocco

Morgan (Welsh)
•dweller on the sea, great, bright

Moris (Greek)
•son of the dark one

Morse (English)
•son of Maurice

Mortimer (French)
•ever living, still water

Morton (Old English)
•from the moor village

Moses (Hebrew, Egyptian)
•saved from the water, son, child

Mosi (Swahili)
•first-born

Murdock (Celtic)
•prosperous seaman

Murphy (Irish)
•sea warrior

Murray (Celtic)
•seaman

Myles (Latin)
•soldier

Myron (Greek)
•fragrant, perfume

Napoleon (Greek, Italian)
•lion from the forest, from Naples, Italy

Narcissus (Greek)
•self-loving, daffodil

Nash (Uncertain)
•alert, active

Nasim (Persian)
•breeze, fresh air

Nasser (Arabic)
•victorious

Nathan (Hebrew)
•a gift

Nathaniel (Hebrew)
•gift of God

Navarro (Spanish)
•plains

N

N

Navin (Hindi)
•new, novel

Nazareth (Hebrew)
•born in Nazareth, Israel

Nehru (Hindi)
•canal

Neil (Celtic, Irish)
•a champion, passionate, cloud, chief

Neka (Native American)
•wild goose

Nelson (Celtic)
•son of Neal

Nemo (Greek)
•glen, glade

Nen (Egyptian)
•ancient waters

Neptune (Latin)
•sea ruler

Nero (Latin, Spanish)
•black, stern

Nestor (Greek)
•venerable wisdom, traveler

Neville (Latin, French)
•from the new town

Nevin (Irish, English)
•nephew, holy, bone, middle; herb

Newell (English)
•new hall

Newland (English)
•new land

Newman (English)
•newcomer

Nicholas (Greek)
•victorious among the people

Nigel (Latin)
•dark

Nikiti (Native American)
•round and smooth like an abalone shell

Niles (English)
•son of Neil

Nimrod (Hebrew)
•rebel

Nino (Spanish)
•young child

Nissan (Hebrew)
•sign, omen; miracle

Nixon (English)
•son of Nick

Noah (Hebrew)
•rest, comfort

Noam (Hebrew)
•sweet, friend

Noble (Latin)
•born to nobility

Nodin (Native American)
•wind

Noel (French, Latin)
•Christmas, birth

Nolan (Celtic, Irish)
•noble or famous, shout

Norbert (Teutonic, Scandinavian)
•shining in the north, brilliant hero

Norman (Old English)
•man from the north

Northrop (English)
•north farm

Norton (Anglo-Saxon)
•from the north place

Nyle (English)
•island

Octavius (Latin)
•the eighth

Odysseus (Greek)
•wrathful

Ogden (Old English)
•from the oak valley

Olaf (Scandinavian)
•peace, ancestor

Oleg (Latvian, Russian)
•holy

Olin (English)
•holly

Oliver (Latin, German)
•peaceful, elf-host

Omar (Arabic, Hebrew)
•thriving, expressive, eloquent, reverent

Oral (Latin)
•verbal, speaker

Oren (Hebrew, Irish)
•pine, green

Orestes (Greek)
•mountain man

Orion (Greek)
•son of fire

Orlando (German)
•famous throughout the land

Ormond (Teutonic, English)
•ship man, bear mountain, spear protector

Orrin (English)
•river

Orson (Latin)
•bear

Orville (French)
•lord of the manor, golden village

Osborn (Anglo-Saxon)
•divinely strong, divine bear

Oscar (Old English)
•spear of a deity

Osmond (Teutonic)
•protected by God

Osric (English)
•divine ruler

Oswald (Anglo-Saxon)
•divine power

Otis (Greek)
•keen of hearing

Otto (Teutonic)
•prosperous

Owen (Celtic, Welsh)
•young warrior

Page (French)
•servant to the royal court

Paki (African)
•witness

Paine (Latin)
•country man or rustic

Palmer (Old English)
•palm bearer

P

Panas (Russian)
•immortal

Paris (Greek)
•lover

Park (Old English, Chinese)
•keeper of the park, cypress tree

Parry (French)
•guardian, protector

Pascal (Hebrew)
•pass over

Patrick (Latin)
•noble, patrician

Patterson (Irish)
•son of Pat

Paul (Latin)
•small

Payne (Latin)
•man from the country

Pearson (English)
•son of Peter

Percival (Latin, French)
•piercing, a knight

Perkin (English)
•little Peter

Perry (Old English)
•the pear tree

Perth (Scottish)
•thornbush thicket

Peter (Greek)
•a rock; reliable

Peyton (Old English)
•fighting man's estate

Phelan (Celtic)
•brave as a wolf

Phelps (English)
•son of Phillip

Philip (Greek)
•lover of horses

Phineas (Hebrew)
•oracle

Pitney (English)
•island of the strong-willed man

Pius (Latin)
•pious

Placido (Spanish)
•serene

Plato (Greek)
•broad-shouldered

Polo (Tibetan)
•brave wanderer

Pomeroy (French)
•apple orchard

Porter (Latin)
•doorkeeper, gate keeper

Powell (Celtic)
•alert

Prentice (Latin)
•apprentice, learner

Prescott (Old English)
•of the priest's dwelling

Price (Welsh)
•son of the ardent one

Primo (Italian)
•first, premier quality

Prince (Latin)
•prince, the first, the leader

Prosper (Latin)
•fortunate

Qabil (Arabic)
•able

Quincy (Latin)
•from the fifth son's place

Quinlan (Irish)
•strong, well shaped

Quinn (Celtic)
•the wise

Rad (English, Slavonic)
•advisor, happy

Radcliffe (Old English)
•from the red cliff

Rafael (Hebrew)
•God has healed

Rafferty (Irish)
•prosperous, rich

Rahim (Arabic)
•merciful

Rahul (Arabic)
•traveler

Raine (English)
•lord, wise

Rainer (German)
•counselor

Rajah (Hindi)
•prince, chief

Rakeem (Arabic)
•writer, recorder

Raleigh (Old English)
•from the deer meadow

Ralph (Teutonic)
•wolf in counsel

Ralston (Old English)
•from the house of Ralph

Ramiro (Portuguese, Spanish)
•supreme judge

Ramsey (Teutonic)
•from the ram's island

Rand (English)
•shield, warrior

Randall (Old English)
•wolf-shield

Randolph (Teutonic)
•shielded or advised by wolves

Ransom (Latin, English)
•redeemer, son of the shield

Raphael (Hebrew)
•God has healed

Rapier (French)
•blade-sharp

Rashad (Arabic)
•good spiritual guidance

Rashid (Turkish, Swahili)
•righteous

Ray (Old French)
•kingly

Raymond (Teutonic, English)
•wise protection, mighty

Reading (English)
•son of the red wanderer

Reece (Welsh)
•enthusiastic, stream

R

Reed (Old English)
•red-haired

Reese (Welsh)
•ardor

Reeve (English)
•steward

Reid (Old English)
•reed

Regan (Celtic)
•royal, kingly

Reginald (Teutonic, English)
•wise dominion, powerful force

Remington (English)
•raven estate

Renato (Italian)
•reborn

Renfred (Teutonic)
•peacemaker

Renny (Irish)
•small but strong

Reuben (Hebrew)
•behold, a son!

Rex (Latin)
•king

Reynard (French)
•wise, bold, courageous

Reynold (English)
•king's advisor

Rhett (German)
•reeds

Rhodes (Greek)
•where roses grow

Rian (Irish)
•little king

Rice (English)
•rich, noble

Richard (Teutonic, English)
•mighty protector

Richmond (German)
•powerful protector

Riddock (Irish)
•smooth field

Rider (English)
•horseman

Ridge (English)
•ridge of a cliff

Ridley (English)
•meadow of reeds

Rigel (Arabic)
•foot

Riley (Irish, Middle English)
•valiant, rye field

Ringo (Japanese)
•apple

Rio (Spanish)
•river

Riordan (Irish)
•bard, royal poet

Rip (Dutch)
•ripe, full-grown

Ripley (English)
•meadow near the river

Ritter (German)
•knight, chivalrous

River (Old French, Latin)
•river, of the river bank

Roarke (Irish)
•famous ruler

Robert (Teutonic, Old English)
•bright in fame

Rocco (Italian)
•rock

Rochester (English)
•rocky fortress

Rockland (English)
•rocky land

Rockwell (English)
•rocky spring

Roden (Irish)
•hearty, lively

Roderick (Teutonic)
•famous ruler

Rodman (Teutonic)
•redhead, famous man, hero

Rodney (Teutonic, Old English)
•renowned, island near the clearing

Roe (English)
•roe deer

Rogan (Irish)
•redhead

Roger (Teutonic)
•famous spearman

Roland (Teutonic)
•man from the country

Rolon (Spanish)
•famous wolf

Roman (Latin)
•from Rome, Italy

Romeo (Latin)
•pilgrim to Rome

Romney (Latin, Welsh)
•a Roman, winding river

Ronan (Irish)
•seal

Rondel (French)
•short poem

Roni (Hebrew)
•my song, my joy

Rooney (Irish)
•redhead

Roosevelt (Dutch)
•field of roses

Rory (Celtic, Irish)
•ruddy, red-haired, red king

Rosario (Portuguese)
•rosary

Roscoe (Teutonic)
•from the deer forest

Ross (Latin, Scottish, French)
•mighty steed, rose, peninsula, red

Rosswell (English)
•springtime of roses

Roth (German)
•redhead

Rover (English)
•traveler

Rowan (English)
•tree with red berries

Roy (Latin)
•king

Royce (French)
•son of the king

Rudolph (Teutonic)
•famous wolf

Rudyard (Old English)
•tenacious, pond with red carp, red enclosure

Rufus (Latin)
•red-haired

R

S

Rune (German, Swedish)
•secret

Rush (French)
•redhead

Russell (Anglo-Saxon, French)
•like a fox, red-haired

Rutherford (Old English)
•from the cattle ford

Rutland (Scandinavian)
•red land

Rutley (English)
•red meadow

Ryan (Irish)
•capable, little king

Ryder (Old English)
•horseman

Safari (Swahili)
•born while traveling

Salvador (Latin, Spanish)
•of the Savior

Samson (Hebrew)
•like the sun

Samuel (Hebrew)
•name of God, heard God,
asked of God

Sanders (Greek)
•helper of mankind

Sanford (Old English)
•from the sandy ford

Santana (Spanish)
•a revolutionary general
and president of Mexico

Sargent (Old French, Latin)
•military attendant, server,
attendant

Sasson (Hebrew)
•joyful

Saul (Hebrew)
•asked for

Sawyer (Celtic, English)
•cutter of timber,
wood worker

Sayer (Welsh)
•carpenter

Schafer (German)
•shepherd

Scorpio (Latin)
•dangerous, deadly

Scott (Old English)
•wanderer, a Scotsman

Scully (Irish)
•town crier

Sean (Hebrew)
•God is gracious

Sebastian (Greek, Latin)
•respected, venerable

Seger (English)
•sea spear, sea warrior

Segundo (Spanish)
•second

Seibert (English)
•bright sea

Selby (Teutonic)
•from the manor farm

Senior (French)
•lord

Sergio (Spanish, Italian)
•servant

S

Seth (Hebrew)
•the chosen or appointed,
to put, set

Sewell (Teutonic)
•victorious on the sea,
mighty in victory

Sexton (English)
•church official, sexton

Seymour (Teutonic, Old French)
•famed at sea, from St. Maur,
prayer

Shad (Punjabi, Persian)
•happy-go-lucky, king

Shamir (Hebrew)
•precious stone

Shannon (Celtic, Irish)
•the ancient god,
small and wise

Shaquille (Arabic)
•handsome

Sharif (Arabic)
•honest, noble

Sharron (Hebrew)
•flat area, plain

Shaw (Old English)
•from the shady grove

Shea (Irish)
•hawk-like, stately, courteous

Sheehan (Irish)
•little, peaceful

Sheffield (English)
•crooked field

Shelby (Anglo-Saxon)
•from the ledge farm

Sheridan (Celtic)
•wild man

Sherlock (Old English)
•fair-haired son

Sherman (Anglo-Saxon)
•wool-shearer or cutter

Sherwin (Anglo-Saxon)
•a true friend, swift runner

Sherwood (Old English)
•from the bright forest

Siddhartha (Hindi)
•original name of Buddha

Sidney (French, Old English)
•follower of St. Denis,
wide, well-watered land

Siegfried (Teutonic)
•victorious peace

Sierra (Irish, Spanish)
•black, saw toothed

Sigmund (Teutonic)
•victorious protection

Silas (Latin)
•of the woods

Simba (Swahili)
•lion

Simon (Hebrew, Greek)
•obedient, he heard,
snub nose

Sinclair (Latin, French)
•illustrious, prayer

Skeeter (English)
•swift

Skelly (Irish)
•storyteller

Skipper (Scandinavian)
•shipmaster

Slade (English)
•child of the valley

S

Slane (Czech)
•salty

Slater (English)
•roof slater

Sloan (Celtic)
•warrior

Snowden (English)
•snowy hill

Socrates (Greek)
•wise, learned

Sol (Latin)
•the sun

Solomon (Hebrew)
•peaceable

Solon (Greek)
•wise

Somerset (English)
•place of the summer settlers

Spencer (Old English, Latin)
•storekeeper

Spike (English)
•ear of grain, long nail

Spiro (Greek)
•round basket, breath

Sprague (Old English)
•alert, quick

Squire (English)
•knight's assistant, large landholder

Stacey (Latin)
•stable, dependable

Stacy (Greek)
•fruitful

Standish (Old English)
•from the stony park

Stanfield (Old English)
•from the stony field

Stanhope (Old English)
•from the stony hollow

Stanislaus (Slavonic)
•glory of the camp

Stanley (Old English)
•dweller by the stony sea, stony meadow

Stanton (Anglo-Saxon)
•from the stone dwelling, ston farm

Starbuck (English)
•challenger of fate

Stark (German)
•strong, vigorous

Steadman (English)
•owner of a farmstead

Steel (English)
•like steel

Stephen (Greek)
•crown

Sterling (Teutonic, English)
•good value, genuine, a starling

Stewart (Anglo-Saxon)
•keeper of the estate

Stillman (Anglo-Saxon)
•quiet, gentle

Stillwell (Anglo-Saxon)
•from the still spring

Sting (English)
•spike of grain

Stockton (English)
•tree-stump town

Stoker (English)
•furnace tender

Stone (English)
•stone

Storr (Norwegian)
•great

Stowe (English)
•hidden, packed away

Stratton (Scottish)
•river valley town

Strom (German, Greek)
•stream, bed, mattress

Strong (English)
•powerful

Stuart (English)
•caretaker

Styles (English)
•stairs put over a wall to help cross it

Sullivan (Irish)
•black eyed

Sully (French, English)
•stain, tarnish, south meadow

Summit (English)
•peak, top

Sumner (Old French, Latin)
•summoner, church official

Sutcliff (English)
•southern cliff

Sutherland (Scandinavian)
•southern land

Sutton (Old English)
•from the south village or town

Sven (Scandinavian)
•youth

Swaine (Teutonic, English)
•boy, herdsman, knight's attendant

Sweeney (Irish)
•small hero

Sylvester (Latin)
•woody, rural, forest dweller

Taber (Old French)
•herald

Tad (Welsh)
•father

Taft (English)
•river

Taggart (Irish)
•son of the priest

Talbert (German)
•bright valley

Talbott (Anglo-Saxon, French)
•bloodhound, boot maker

Talib (Arabic)
•seeker

Talon (French, English)
•claw, nail

Tam (Hebrew, Vietnamese)
•honest, number eight

Tamson (Scandinavian)
•son of Thomas

Tan (Burmese, Vietnamese)
•million, new

Tanek (Greek)
•immortal

Tanner (Old English)
•hide tanner

Tano (Spanish, Ghanian)
•camp glory, a river in Ghana

T

Tarrant (Welsh)
•thunder

Tate (Scandinavian)
•cheerful, long-winded

Tavis (Celtic)
•son of David

Tavor (Aramaic)
•misfortune

Taylor (Latin, French)
•a tailor

Teague (Celtic)
•poet

Teller (English)
•storyteller

Tembo (Swahili)
•elephant

Templeton (English)
•town near the temple

Terrence (Latin)
•tender, polished

Terrill (Teutonic)
•martial, belonging to Thor,
thunder ruler

Tertius (Latin)
•the third

Teva (Hebrew)
•nature

Thaddeus (Hebrew, Greek, Latin)
•praise to God, courageous

Thane (English)
•attendant warrior

Thatcher (Anglo-Saxon)
•mender of roofs

Thayer (Teutonic)
•of the nation's army

Theobald (German)
•people's prince

Theodore (Greek)
•gift of God

Thomas (Hebrew, Aramaic)
•the twin, good company

Thor (Scandinavian)
•thunderous one

Thorgood (English)
•Thor is good

Thornton (Anglo-Saxon)
•from the thorn tree place

Thorpe (Anglo-Saxon)
•from the small village

Thurston (Scandinavian)
•Thor's stone

Tibor (Hungarian)
•holy place

Tiernan (Irish)
•lord

Tiger (American)
•tiger, powerful and energetic

Tilden (Old English)
•from the fertile valley

Timon (Greek)
•honorable

Timothy (Greek)
•revering God

Titus (Latin, Greek)
•saved, hero, giant

Tivon (Hebrew)
•nature lover

Tobias (Hebrew)
•God's goodness

Todd (Latin, Old English)
•the fox

Tomlin (English)
•little Tom

Tong (Vietnamese)
•fragrant

Tony (Greek, Latin)
•flourishing, praiseworthy

Torr (English)
•tower

Torrence (Irish)
•knolls

Tracey (Anglo-Saxon, Greek)
•brave defender, harvester,
battler

Trader (English)
•well-trodden path, skilled
worker

Trahern (Celtic)
•stronger than iron

Travell (English)
•traveler

Travis (French, Latin, English)
•from the crossroad, toll,
toll collector

Tremain (Celtic)
•from the town of the
stone

Trent (Latin, Celtic, French)
•swift, flooder, thirty

Trevor (Celtic, Welsh)
•prudent traveler, great
homestead

Trigg (Scandinavian)
•trusty

Trip (English)
•traveler

Tristan (Latin, Celtic, Welsh)
•sorrowful, tumult, loud noise,
bold

Troy (English, Irish, French)
•foot soldier, curly haired,
water

True (English)
•faithful, loyal

Trustin (English)
•trustworthy

Tucker (Old English)
•to torment, to stretch, fabric
pleater, fuller

Tudor (Greek)
•divine gift

Tupper (English)
•ram raiser

Turner (Latin)
•worker with the lathe, wood-
worker

Tut (Arabic)
•strong and courageous

Twain (English)
•divided in two

Tyler (Old English)
•maker of tiles

Tynan (Irish)
•dark

Tyrel (Middle English, French)
•stubborn

Tyrone (Irish, Greek)
•Owen's territory, sovereign

Tyson (Teutonic, Old French)
•son of the German, firebrand

T

U/V

Ulan (African)
•first-born twin

Ulmer (English)
•famous wolf

Ulric (Teutonic)
•ruler of all

Ulysses (Latin, Greek)
•venturer, wrathful

Unika (Lomwe)
•brighten

Upton (Anglo-Saxon)
•from the high town, upper forest

Urban (Latin)
•from the city, sophisticated

Urian (Greek)
•from heaven

Uriel (Hebrew)
•flame of God

Vale (French, Latin)
•from the valley

Valentine (Latin)
•health, strong, valorous

Vance (Teutonic, Old English)
•son of a famous family, marshes

Vaughan (Celtic)
•small or little

Vernon (Latin, French)
•flourishing, alder-tree, springlike, youthful

Victor (Latin)
•conqueror

Vincent (Latin)
•conquering one

Virgil (Latin)
•strong, flourishing

Vito (Latin)
•vital

Vivien (Latin)
•lively

Vladimir (Slavonic)
•world ruler

Wade (Anglo-Saxon)
•wanderer, river ford

Wadsworth (Old English)
•from Wade's castle, village near the ford

Wagner (German)
•wagoner, wagon-maker

Waite (English)
•watchman

Walcott (Old English)
•dweller in the walled cottage

Walker (Old English)
•forester, one who walks on wool, cloth cleaner

Wallace (Teutonic)
•foreigner, Welshman

Waller (German, English)
•powerful, wall maker

Walter (Teutonic, English)
•powerful, of great destiny

Wang (Chinese)
•hope, wish

Ward (Anglo-Saxon)
•guardian

Warren (Teutonic, French)
•protecting friend, game park

Warwick (Teutonic)
•strong ruler

Washington (English)
•purifying, town near water

Watkins (English)
•son of Walter

Watson (Anglo-Saxon)
•warrior's son

Waverly (English)
•quaking aspen-tree meadow

Wayland (Old English)
•from the land by the highway

Wayman (English)
•road man, traveler

Wayne (Old English)
•wagon-maker

Webster (Old English)
•weaver

Wellington (Anglo-Saxon)
•from the prosperous estate

Wells (Old English)
•dweller by the spring

Wendell (Teutonic, English)
•wanderer, good dale

Wesley (Anglo-Saxon)
•from the west meadow

West (English)
•west

Weston (Old English)
•from the west village

Weylin (Celtic)
•son of the wolf

Wheeler (English)
•wheel maker, wagon driver

Whistler (English)
•whistler, piper

Whitman (English)
•white-haired man

Whitmore (English)
•white moor

Whitney (Anglo-Saxon)
•from the white island

Wilber (Anglo-Saxon)
•inventive, wall fortification, bright willows

Wilbert (German)
•brilliant, resolute

Wiley (English)
•willow meadow

Willard (Old English, German)
•protecting, bold resolve

William (Teutonic, English)
•determined protector, helmet

Willoughby (English)
•willow farm

Wilmer (Teutonic)
•beloved and famous

Wilmot (Teutonic)
•beloved heart, resolute spirit

Wilson (Teutonic)
•son of William

W/X

Wilton (Old English)
•from the farmstead by the spring

Win (Cambodian)
•bright

Winchell (Anglo-Saxon)
•drawer of water

Winfield (Anglo-Saxon)
•from the friendly field

Winfred (Teutonic)
•joyous peace

Wing (Chinese)
•glory

Wingate (English)
•winding gate

Winslow (Anglo-Saxon)
•friendly, friend's hill

Winston (Anglo-Saxon)
•from the friendly town

Winter (English)
•born in winter

Winthrop (Anglo-Saxon)
•from the friendly village, victory at the crossroads

Witter (English)
•wise warrior

Wolcott (English)
•cottage in the woods

Wolfgang (Teutonic)
•path of a wolf, wolf quarrel

Woodrow (Old English)
•from the hedgerow by the forest

Woodward (Old English)
•keeper of the forest

Woolsey (English)
•victorious wolf

Worcester (English)
•forest army camp

Worthington (Anglo-Saxon)
•from the riverside

Wray (Scandinavian, English)
•corner property, crooked

Wren (Welsh, English)
•chief, ruler, wren

Wright (Old English)
•craftsman

Wyatt (Old English, French, German)
•guide, little warrior, wide

Wycliff (English)
•white cliff, village near the cliff

Wylie (Anglo-Saxon)
•beguiling

Wyman (Anglo-Saxon)
•warrior

Wyndham (Old English)
•from the windy village

Wynne (Welsh, English)
•intuitive, sympathetic, light-skinned, friend

Wythe (English)
•willow tree

Xanthus (Latin)
•golden haired

Xavier (Arabic, Basque)
•brilliant, new house

Xenos (Greek)
•stronger, strange guest

Xerxes (Persian)
•king

Yale (Teutonic, Welsh, English)
•payer, fertile upland, old

Yardley (Old English)
•from the enclosed meadow

Yaron (Hebrew)
•he will sing, he will cry out

Yasir (Afghani, Arabic)
•humble, takes it easy, wealth

Yavin (Hebrew)
•he will understand

York (Latin, English)
•sacred tree, boar estate, yew-tree estate

Yoshio (Japanese)
•good, respectful

Yule (English)
•born at Christmas

Yuli (Basque)
•youthful

Yves (French)
•an archer

Zachary (Hebrew)
•God remembered

Zahir (Arabic)
•shining, bright

Zane (Danish, German, English)
•tenth, sea friend

Zaki (Arabic, Hausa)
•bright, pure, lion

Zale (Greek)
•sea strength

Zan (Italian)
•clown

Zareb (African)
•protector

Zared (Hebrew)
•ambush

Zarek (Polish)
•my God protect the king

Zeki (Turkish)
•clever, intelligent

Zelig (Teutonic)
•blessed

Zeus (Greek)
•living, king of the Greek gods

Zoltan (Hungarian)
•sultan, ruler

Zorba (Greek)
•live each day

Yamuna (Hindi)
•sacred river

Yang (Chinese)
•sun

Yen (Chinese)
•yearning, desirous

Yeo (Korean)
•mild

Yepa (Native American)
•snow girl

Yesenia (Arabic)
•flower

Yetta (Teutonic)
•mistress of the house

Yoko (Japanese)
•positive, good girl

Yolanda (Latin, Greek)
•modest, shy, violet flower

Yuri (Japanese)
•lily

Yvonne (French, German)
•the archer, yew wood, bow wood

Zabrina (Anglo-Saxon)
•of the nobility

Zada (Arabic)
•fortunate, prosperous

Zandra (Greek)
•helper of mankind

Zea (Latin)
•grain

Zelda (Teutonic)
•gray-haired battle maiden

Zelene (English)
•sunshine

Zemirah (Hebrew)
•song of joy

Zena (Greek, Ethiopian)
•hospitable, news, woman

Zenia (Greek)
•having life from Jupiter

Zephr (Greek)
•west wind

Zeta (English, Portuguese)
•rose

Zhen (Chinese)
•chaste

Zia (Arabic)
•night

Zinah (Hebrew)
•abundance

Zinnia (Latin)
•plant with beautiful, rayed, colorful flowers

Zita (Greek, Spanish, Arabic)
•harvester, rose, mistress

Zoe (Greek)
•life

Zola (Italian)
•piece of earth

Zora (Latin, Slavonic)
•dawn, aurora

W/X

Viola (Latin)
•violet, stringed instrument in violin family

Violet (Latin)
•shy, modest

Virginia (Latin)
•pure, chaste

Vivian (Latin)
•lively

Walker (English)
•cloth, walker

Wallis (Teutonic)
•girl of Wales

Wanda (Teutonic)
•wanderer

Waneta (Native American)
•charger

Weeko (Native American)
•pretty girl

Wendy (Welsh)
•white, light skinned

Wenona (Native American)
•the first born

Weslee (English)
•western meadow

Whitney (Old English)
•white island

Whoopi (English)
•happy, excited

Wilda (German, English)
•untamed wild one, willow

Wilfreda (Teutonic)
•resolute peacemaker

Wilhelmina (Teutonic)
•protectress

Willa (Anglo-Saxon)
•desired, desirable

Willow (English)
•willow tree

Wilma (Teutonic)
•determined

Wilona (English)
•desired

Winifred (Teutonic)
•friend of peace

Winna (African)
•friend

Winter (English)
•winter

Wynne (Celtic)
•fair, white

Wyoming (Native American)
•western American state

Xanthe (Greek)
•blond

Xaviera (Basque, Arabic)
•new house, bright

Xela (Quiche)
•my mountain home

Xena (Greek)
•hospitable

Xiang (Chinese)
•fragrant

Xylia (Greek)
•of the wood

Uma (Hindi)
• mother

Umeko (Japanese)
• plum blossom child, patient

Una (Latin, Native American)
• the one, good memory

Undine (Latin)
• water nymph, little wave

Unity (Middle English)
• oneness

Uria (Hebrew)
• light of the Lord

Urika (Omaha)
• useful to everyone

Ursula (Latin)
• little she-bear

Uta (German, Japanese)
• rich, poem

Valentina (Latin)
• vigorous

Valerie (Latin)
• strong

Valonia (Latin)
• shadow valley

Vanessa (Greek)
• butterfly

Vania (Hebrew)
• God's gracious gift

Vanity (English)
• vain

Vanna (Cambodian)
• golden

Vanora (Welsh)
• white wave

Varda (Hebrew)
• rose

Veda (Sanskrit)
• wise

Vega (Arabic)
• falling star

Velda (Teutonic)
• of great wisdom

Velma (Teutonic)
• warm-hearted

Velvet (English)
• velvety

Venus (Latin)
• love, planet

Vera (Russian, Latin)
• faith, true

Verna (Latin)
• spring-born

Veronica (Latin)
• true image

Vesta (Latin)
• guardian of the sacred fire

Victoria (Latin)
• victorious

Vida (Hebrew, Latin)
• beloved

Vina (Hindi)
• musical instrument played by Hindu goddess of wisdom

Vincentia (Latin)
• victor, conqueror

Vinna (Old English)
• of the vine

U

Tierney (Irish)
•lord, noble

Tiffany (Greek)
•revelation of God

Tipper (Irish)
•water pourer

Tira (Hindi)
•arrow

Tirza (Hebrew)
•pleasant

Tisa (Swahili)
•ninth-born

Tita (Greek)
•giant

Tobey (Hebrew)
•God is good

Toki (Japanese)
•hopeful

Tomi (Japanese)
•rich

Toni (Greek, Latin)
•flourishing, praiseworthy

Tonia (Latin, Slavonic)
•beyond praise, fairy queen

Topaz (Latin)
•golden yellow gem

Topsy (English)
•on top

Tora (Japanese)
•tiger

Tori (Japanese)
•bird

Tory (English)
•victorious

Tosha (Punjabi)
•armaments

Tracey (Latin)
•warrior

Treasure (Latin, Middle English)
•storehouse, wealth

Trilby (English)
•soft hat

Trina (Hindi)
•points of sacred kusa grass

Trinity (Latin)
•triad

Trisha (Hindi)
•thirsty

Trista (Latin)
•sorrowful

Tristen (Latin)
•bold

Tuesday (English)
•second day of the week

Tula (Hindi)
•born in the month of Capricor

Turquoise (French)
•blue green, semiprecious stone

Tyler (English)
•tailor

Tyne (English)
•river

Tyra (Scandinavian)
•battler

Ulani (Polynesian)
•cheerful

Ulla (German, Swedish)
•willful

Talitha (Arabic)
•young girl

Tallis (French, English)
•forest

Tallulah (Choctaw)
•leaping water

Tam (Vietnamese)
•heart

Tama (Japanese)
•jewel

Tameka (Aramaic)
•twin

Tamiko (Japanese)
•child of the people

Tandy (English)
•team

Tani (Japanese, Slavonic)
•valley, stand of glory

Tanisha (African, Arabic)
•born on a Monday, woman

Tanya (Russian)
•fairy queen

Tara (Celtic)
•tower

Tasha (Greek)
•born on Christmas day

Tashi (Hausa)
•bird in flight

Tatum (Old English)
•cheerful

Taura (Latin)
•bull

Tavie (Scottish)
•twin

Tawny (Middle English, Gypsy)
•yellowish brown, little one

Taylor (Middle English)
•tailor

Teagan (Welsh)
•beautiful, attractive

Teal (English)
•river duck, blue green

Tempest (Latin)
•weather, storm

Tera (Latin, Japanese)
•earth, swift arrow

Teresa (Greek)
•harvester, reaper

Thea (Greek)
•goddess

Thelma (Greek)
•nurse, willful

Thema (African)
•queen

Theodora (Greek)
•divine gift

Thera (Greek)
•untamed

Theta (Greek)
•letter in Greek alphabet

Thomasina (Hebrew)
•the twin

Tia (Spanish, Greek)
•aunt, princess

Tiara (Greek, Latin)
•turban, headdress, jeweled coronet

Tiberia (Latin)
•Tiber River in Italy

Tida (Thai)
•daughter

Sonya (Greek)
•wise

Sophia (Greek)
•wisdom

Sora (Native American)
•chirping songbird

Soraya (Persian)
•princess

Sorrel (French)
•reddish brown

Spring (English)
•springtime

Stacy (Greek)
•resurrection

Starling (English)
•bird

Starr (English)
•star

Stella (Latin)
•star

Stephanie (Greek)
•crown

Stockard (English)
•stockyard

Stormy (English)
•impetuous by nature

Sugar (American)
•sweet as sugar

Suki (Japanese, Moquelumnan)
•loved one, eagle-eyed

Sula (Icelandic)
•large seabird

Sumi (Japanese)
•elegant, refined

Summer (Old English)
•summer

Sunee (Thai)
•good

Suni (Zuni)
•native, member of our tribe

Sunny (English)
•bright, cheerful

Suri (Todas)
•pointy nose

Surya (Pakistani)
•sun god

Susan (Hebrew)
•lily

Sybil (Greek)
•prophetess

Sydel (Hebrew)
•enchantress

Sydney (Hebrew)
•the enticer

Sylvia (Latin)
•forest maiden

Tabitha (Aramaic, Greek)
a gazelle

Tabia (Swahili)
•talented

Tabina (Arabic)
•follower of Muhammed

Taffy (Welsh)
•beloved

Tala (Native American)
•stalking wolf

Talia (Greek, Hebrew, French)
•blooming, dew from heaven

S

Shamira (Hebrew)
•precious stone

Shana (Hebrew)
•God is gracious

Shanley (Irish)
•hero's child

Shannon (Celtic, Irish)
•the ancient god, old one, small and wise

Sharan (Hindi)
•protector

Shari (French)
•beloved, dearest

Sharik (African)
•child of God

Sharon (Hebrew)
•of the land of Sharon

Shayna (Hebrew)
•beautiful

Shea (Irish)
•fairy place

Sheila (Celtic, Latin)
•musical, blind

Shelby (Old English)
•land on the edge, willow village

Shelley (Old English)
•clearing on a ledge

Shenandoah (Native American)
•spruce stream

Shilo (Hebrew)
•God's gift

Shina (Japanese)
•virtuous

Shira (Hebrew)
•song

Shirley (Anglo-Saxon)
•from the white meadow

Shoshana (Hebrew)
•lily

Shulamith (Hebrew)
•peaceful

Sibley (English)
•sibling, friendly

Sidonia (Hebrew)
•enticing

Sierra (Spanish, Irish)
•saw-tooth mountain range, black

Signe (Latin)
•sign, signal

Sigourney (English)
•victorious conqueror

Simone (Hebrew)
•heard by the Lord

Sirena (Greek)
•enchanter

Skye (Arabic)
•water giver

Skyler (Dutch)
•sheltering

Sloane (Irish)
•warrior

Solana (Spanish)
•sunshine

Solange (French)
•dignified

Soma (Hindi)
•lunar

Sommer (Arabic)
•black

S

Sage (English)
•wise

Sahara (Arabic)
•desert, wilderness

Sala (Hindi)
•sala tree

Salama (Arabic)
•peaceful

Salena (Greek, French)
•salty, solemn, dignified

Salima (Arabic)
•safe and sound, healthy

Sally (English)
•princess

Salome (Hebrew)
•woman of perfection, peace

Salvadora (Spanish)
•savior

Samantha (Hebrew, Arabic)
•told by God, listener

Samara (Hebrew, Latin)
•watchful, cautious, elm tree seed

Sandra (Greek)
•helper of mankind

Santana (Spanish)
•saint

Sanya (Sanskrit)
•born on Saturday

Sapphire (Greek)
•blue gemstone

Sara (Japanese)
•assistant

Sarah (Hebrew)
•princess

Saree (Arabic)
•noble

Savannah (Caribbean, Spanish)
•meadow, treeless plain

Sawa (Native American)
•rock

Scarlett (Middle English)
•deep red

Scotti (Scottish)
•from Scotland

Sebastiane (Greek, Latin)
•venerable, revered

Seema (Greek, Afghani)
•sprout, sky, profile

Seki (Japanese)
•wonderful

Selam (Ethiopian)
•peaceful

Selena (Greek)
•moon goddess

Selima (Hebrew)
•peaceful

Selma (Celtic, German)
•fair, secure

Seraphine (Hebrew)
•deeply religious, burning, ardent

Serena (Latin)
•tranquil

Sevilla (Spanish)
•from Seville

Shahla (Afghani)
•beautiful eyes

Shafira (Swahili)
•distinguished

Rory (Irish)
•famous brilliance

Rosabel (Latin)
•beautiful rose

Rosalie (Latin)
•festival of roses

Rosamond (German)
•famous guardian

Roslyn (Latin, Spanish)
•fair rose

Rosanne (Latin)
•gracious rose

Rose (Latin)
•rose

Rosemarie (Latin)
•Mary's rose

Roshan (Sanskrit)
•shining light

Rowan (English)
•tree with red berries

Rowena (Celtic, Old English)
•flowing fair hair,
famous friend

Roxanne (Persian)
•dawn

Royale (English)
•royal

Ruana (Hindi)
•stringed musical instrument

Ruby (Old French)
•red

Rudee (German)
•famous wolf

Rue (German, French, English)
•famous, street, regretful,
strong-scented herbs

Rula (Latin, English)
•ruler

Ruri (Japanese)
•emerald

Ruta (Lithuanian)
•rue

Ruth (Hebrew)
•friend

Ryann (Irish)
•little ruler

Ryba (Czech)
•fish

Rylee (Irish)
•valiant

Ryo (Japanese)
•dragon

Saba (Arabic)
•morning

Sable (English)
•sable, sleek

Sabra (Hebrew)
•thorny cactus fruit

Sabrina (Anglo-Saxon, Latin)
•a princess, boundary line

Sacha (Greek)
•helpmate

Sachi (Japanese)
•blessed, lucky

Sada (Japanese)
•chaste

Sade (Yoruba)
•honor confers a crown

R

Renita (Latin)
•poised, firm

Reseda (Spanish)
•fragrant mignonette blossom

Reta (African)
•shaken

Reubena (Hebrew)
•behold a daughter

Reva (Latin, Hebrew)
•revived, rain, one-fourth

Rexanne (American)
•queen

Reyhan (Turkish)
•sweet-smelling flower

Rhea (Greek)
•motherly, brook, stream

Rhiannon (Celtic, Welsh)
•great queen, witch, nymph, goddess

Rhoda (Greek)
•rose, from Rhodes

Rhona (Scottish)
•powerful, mighty

Rhonda (Celtic, Welsh)
•noisy one, grand

Ria (Spanish)
•river

Ricarda (Spanish)
•rich and powerful ruler

Richael (Irish)
•saint

Rika (Swedish)
•ruler

Riley (Irish)
•valiant

Rima (Arabic)
•white antelope

Rimona (Hebrew)
•pomegranate

Rinah (Hebrew)
•joyful

Riona (Irish)
•saint

Risa (Latin)
•laughter

Risha (Hindi)
•born during the lunar month of Taurus

Rita (Greek, Sanskrit)
•pearl, brave, honest

Riva (Old French)
•dreamer, river bank

Roanna (Latin)
•sweet, gracious

Roberta (Anglo-Saxon)
•of shining fame

Robin (English)
•robin

Rochelle (French)
•little rock, large stone

Roderica (Teutonic)
•princess, famous ruler

Rohana (Sanskrit, Hindi)
•sandalwood

Rolanda (Teutonic)
•famous

Roma (Latin)
•woman of Rome

Ronalda (Teutonic)
•powerful

Quinta (Latin, English)
•fifth child, queen's lawn

Quintessa (Latin)
•essence

Quirita (Latin)
•citizen

Quisha (African)
•excellence of mind

Rabi (Arabic)
•breeze

Rachel (Hebrew)
•ewe, motherly

Radclyffe (Middle English)
•red cliff

Rae (English)
•doe

Rafa (Arabic)
•happy, prosperous

Raina (German)
•mighty

Rainbow (English)
•rainbow

Raja (Arabic)
•hopeful

Raku (Japanese)
•pleasure

Rama (Hebrew, Hindi)
•lofty, exalted, godlike

Ramona (Teutonic, Spanish)
•protector, mighty

Ran (Japanese, Scandinavian)
•water lily, destroyer

Rana (Sanskrit, Arabic)
•royal, gaze, look

Randall (English)
•protected

Randi (Old English)
•shield-wolf

Rani (Sanskrit, Hebrew)
•queen, joyful

Ranita (Hebrew)
•song

Raphaela (Hebrew)
•blessed healer, healed by God

Rasha (Arabic)
•young gazelle

Raven (English)
•blackbird, raven

Raya (Hebrew)
•friend

Rea (Greek)
•poppy flower

Rebba (Hebrew)
•fourth child

Rebecca (Hebrew)
•tie, bond

Reena (Greek)
•peaceful

Regan (Irish)
•descendant of a small ruler

Regina (Latin, English)
•queenly, king's advisor

Rena (Hebrew)
•song

Renee (French)
•reborn

Petunia (Native American)
•flower

Philana (Greek)
•friend of mankind

Philantha (Greek)
•lover of flowers

Philippa (Greek)
•lover of horses

Philomena (Greek)
•loving friend, love song

Phoebe (Greek)
•shining

Phyllis (Greek)
•green leaf

Pia (Latin)
•devout

Pilar (Spanish)
•pillar, column

Piper (English)
•pipe player

Pippi (French)
•rosy cheeked

Pita (African)
•fourth daughter

Poni (African)
•second daughter

Poppy (Latin)
•poppy flower

Portia (Latin)
•doorway, offering

Precious (Latin, French)
•valuable, costly, dear

Prima (Latin)
•first born

Primavera (Italian, Spanish)
•spring

Primrose (Latin)
•first rose

Princess (English)
•daughter of royalty

Priscilla (Latin)
•of long lineage

Prudence (Latin)
•prudent

Prunella (Latin)
•brown, little plum

Psyche (Greek)
•soul

Purity (English)
•purity

Qadira (Arabic)
•powerful

Qamra (Arabic)
•moon

Qitarah (Arabic)
•fragrant

Qubilah (Arabic)
•agreeable

Querida (Spanish)
•loved one

Questra (Latin, French)
•seeker, searcher

Quinby (Scandinavian)
•queen's estate

Quincy (Irish)
•fifth

Quinn (German, English)
•queen

Ophelia (Greek)
•wise

Oprah (Hebrew)
•runaway

Oriana (Latin, Irish)
•golden, dawn, sunrise

Orinda (Hebrew, Irish)
•pine tree, light skinned, white

Oriole (Latin)
•golden, black and orange bird

Orla (Irish)
•golden princess

Orlanda (German)
•famous throughout the land

Orlena (Latin)
•golden

Ormanda (Latin, German)
noble, mariner, seaman

Osanna (Latin)
•praise the Lord

Owena (Welsh)
•nobility, young warrior

Oz (Hebrew)
•strength

Paige (Anglo-Saxon)
•young, child

Paisley (Scottish)
•patterned fabric made in Paisley, Scotland

Paloma (Spanish)
•dove

Pamela (Greek)
•honey, loving

Pandora (Greek)
•gifted

Pansy (French, Greek)
•thought, flower, fragrant

Paris (French)
•capital of France

Pascale (French)
•born on Easter or Passover

Patia (Gypsy, Spanish)
•leaf

Patience (Latin)
•patient

Patricia (Latin)
•of the nobility, well-born

Paula (Latin)
•little

Peace (English)
•peaceful

Pearl (English)
•pearl

Penelope (Greek)
•weaver, industrious

Peni (Carrier)
•mind

Peony (Greek)
•flower

Perri (Greek, Latin, French)
•small rock, traveler

Petra (Greek)
•rock

Petrina (Greek)
•steadfast

Petula (Old French)
•peevish

O

Nita (Hebrew, Choctaw)
•planter, bear

Nitza (Hebrew)
•flower bud

Noel (Latin)
•Christmas child

Nola (Celtic, Latin)
•noble, famous, small bell

Noleta (Latin)
•unwilling

Nona (Latin)
•the ninth

Nora (Greek)
•light

Norell (Scandinavian)
•from the north

Nori (Japanese)
•law, tradition

Norma (Latin)
•model, rule, precept

Nova (Latin, Native American)
•new, butterfly chaser

Novella (Latin)
•newcomer

Novia (Spanish)
•sweetheart

Nueva (Spanish)
•new

Nuna (Native American)
•land

Nunciata (Latin)
•messenger

Nura (Aramaic)
•light

Nydia (Latin)
•a refuge, nest

Nyree (Maori)
•sea

Nyssa (Greek)
•beginning

Oceana (Greek)
•ocean

Odelia (French, Latin)
•prosperous, wealth

Odessa (Greek)
•odyssey, long voyage

Odette (French)
•home lover

Oki (Japanese)
•middle of the ocean

Ola (Scandinavian)
•daughter of descendant

Olga (Teutonic)
•holy

Olina (Hawaiian)
•filled with happiness

Olinda (Latin, Spanish)
•scented, protector of property

Olivia (Latin)
•olive, peace-bringer

Olympia (Greek)
•of the mountain of the Gods

Oneida (Native American)
•eagerly awaited

Opal (Hindi)
•precious stone

Nadine (French)
•hope

Naida (Greek)
•water nymph

Nana (Hawaiian)
•spring

Nancy (English)
•gracious

Nani (Hebrew)
•pleasant, beautiful

Naomi (Hebrew)
•pleasant

Nara (Greek, Japanese)
•happy, north, oak

Narcissa (Greek)
•daffodil

Narda (Persian)
•anointed

Narelle (Australian)
•woman from the sea

Nari (Japanese)
•thunder

Natara (Arabic)
•sacrifice

Natalie (Latin)
•child of Christmas

Neda (Slavonic)
•Sunday's child

Nedda (English)
•prosperous, guardian

Neema (Swahili)
•born in prosperous times

Neila (Irish)
•champion

Nelle (Greek)
•stone

Neona (Greek)
•new moon

Nerissa (Greek)
•of the sea

Nessa (Scandinavian)
•promontory

Neta (Hebrew)
•plant, shrub

Neva (English, Russian)
•snow, new, river in Russia

Nevada (Spanish)
•snow

Nevina (Irish)
•worshipper of the saint

Neylan (Turkish)
•fulfilled wish

Nicole (Greek)
•victory of the people

Nida (Omaha)
•an elflike creature

Nika (Russian)
•belonging to God

Nikita (Greek)
•unconquerable

Nima (Hebrew, Arabic)
•thread, blessing

Nina (Spanish)
•little girl

Nisa (Arabic)
•woman

Nissa (Hebrew, Scandinavian)
•sign, emblem, friendly elf

M

Miliani (Hawaiian)
•caress

Millicent (Teutonic)
•strength

Mimi (Teutonic)
•resolute opponent

Mina (German, Hindi, Arabic)
•love, blue sky, harbor

Minerva (Greek)
•wise

Minette (French)
•faithful

Minna (Teutonic)
•loving memory

Mira (Spanish)
•look, gaze

Miranda (Latin)
•to be admired

Mireli (Hebrew)
•God spoke

Miriam (Hebrew)
•bitter, rebellious

Misty (Old English)
•lightly foggy

Miya (Japanese)
•temple

Moira (Irish)
•great

Mona (Irish)
•solidarity, noble one

Monica (Latin, Greek)
•advisor, alone

Montana (Spanish)
•mountain

Mora (Spanish)
•blueberry

Morela (Polish)
•apricot

Morgan (Welsh)
•sea, bright

Moriah (Hebrew, French)
•God is my teacher

Morie (Japanese)
•bay

Morna (Gaelic)
•tender and gentle

Morrisa (Latin)
•dark skinned, moor

Moselle (Hebrew, French)
•drawn from the water, a white wine

Moya (Celtic)
•the great

Mura (Japanese)
•village

Muriel (Hebrew, Irish, Arabic)
•bittersweet, sea-bright

Myla (English)
•merciful

Mylene (Greek)
•dark

Myra (Latin)
•wonderful, fragrant

Myrna (Irish)
•beloved

Myrtle (Greek)
•victorious crown

Mead (Greek)
•honey wine

Meara (Irish)
•mirthful

Meda (Native American)
•prophet, priestess

Medea (Greek, Latin)
•part goddess, middle

Meena (Hinda)
•blue semiprecious stone

Megan (Celtic, Greek)
•the strong, pearl

Megara (Greek)
•first

Megumi (Japanese)
•blessing

Mei (Hawaiian)
•great

Meira (Hebrew)
•light

Mel (Portuguese, Spanish)
•sweet as honey

Melanie (Greek)
•blackness, dark skinned

Melba (Greek, Latin)
•soft, slender, flower

Mele (Hawaiian)
•song, poem

Melina (Latin)
•canary yellow

Melinda (Greek, Latin)
•grateful, honey

Meliora (Latin)
•better

Melissa (Greek)
•honey bee

Melodie (Greek)
•song

Melvina (Celtic)
•chief

Mercedes (Spanish, Latin)
•merciful, reward

Meredith (Celtic)
•protector of the sea

Meri (Finnish)
•sea

Meriel (Irish)
•shining sea

Merle (Latin, French)
•blackbird

Merry (Old English)
•pleasant, merry

Meryl (Latin, German, Irish)
•blackbird, famous, shining

Merritt (Anglo-Saxon)
•of merit

Mia (Latin)
•mine

Michelle (French)
•who is like God

Midori (Japanese)
•green

Mieko (Japanese)
•prosperous

Mignon (Old French)
•dainty, cute, graceful

Mika (Native American)
•God's child, wise raccoon

Mila (Russian)
•dear one

Mildred (Old French, English)
•gentle strength

M

Manda (Spanish)
•woman warrior

Mandeep (Punjabi)
•enlightened

Mandisa (Xhosa)
•sweet

Mansi (Native American-Hopi)
•plucked flower

Marah (Hebrew)
•bitter

Marcia (Latin)
•of Mars

Mardi (French)
•born on Tuesday

Maren (Latin)
•sea

Margaret (Greek)
•a pearl

Mari (Japanese)
•ball

Marigold (English)
•plant with yellow or
orange flowers

Mariko (Japanese)
•circle

Marina (Latin)
•sea maiden

Marini (Swahili)
•health, pretty

Maris (Latin)
•sea star

Marisol (Spanish)
•sunny sea

Mariyan (Arabic)
•purity

Marjolaine (French)
•marjoram

Marlene (Greek)
•high tower

Marnina (Hebrew)
•rejoice

Marquise (French)
•noble-woman

Marsala (Italian)
•from Marseille, Italy

Martha (Aramaic)
•the lady, sorrowful

Martina (Latin)
•belonging to Mars, warlike

Mary (Hebrew)
•bitter, sympathetic

Marya (Arabic)
•purity, bright whiteness

Mathena (Hebrew)
•gift of God

Mathilda (Teutonic)
•courageous

Matsuko (Japanese)
•pine tree

Maureen (Latin, French)
•dark

Mauve (French)
•violet colored

Mavis (Celtic, French)
•songbird

Maxine (Latin)
•the greatest

May (Middle English)
•maiden, great, flower

Mazel (Hebrew)
•lucky

Lurleen (Scandinavian)
•war horn

Lycoris (Greek)
•twilight

Lyda (Slavonic)
•loved by all

Lydia (Greek, Arabic)
•intelligent, strife

Lyla (French)
•island

Lynelle (English)
•pretty

Lynn (Anglo-Saxon)
•cascade, stream, pool

Lyra (Greek)
•lyre player

Lysandra (Greek)
•liberator

Mabel (Latin)
•lovable

Mackenzie (Irish)
•daughter of the wise leader

Madeline (Hebrew, Greek)
•tower of strength

Madison (Middle English)
•son of Matthew, good

Madonna (Latin)
•my lady

Maeko (Japanese)
•honest child

Maeve (Irish)
•intoxicating, joyous

Magdalen (Greek)
•high tower

Maggie (Greek)
•pearl

Magnolia (Latin)
•flowering tree

Mahal (Filipino)
•love

Mahala (Arabic)
•marrow, tender, powerful

Mahogony (Spanish)
•rich, strong

Mai (Japanese, Vietnamese)
•brightness, flower, coyote

Maia (Greek, English)
•mother, nurse, kinswoman

Maida (Anglo-Saxon)
•maiden

Maja (Arabic)
•splendid

Malaya (Filipino)
•free

Malha (Hebrew)
•queen

Mali (Thai)
•jasmine flower

Malika (Hungarian)
•industrious

Malina (Native American)
•soothing

Malini (Hindi)
•gardener

Mallory (Old French)
•the unlucky one

M

Lila (Arabic, Hindi, Persian)
•night, free will of god

Liv (Old Norse)
•defense

Lilian (Latin)
•pure as a lily

Lilith (Hebrew, Arabic)
•evil woman, of the night

Limber (Tiv)
•joyful

Lin (Chinese)
•beautiful

Lina (Greek, Arabic)
•light, tender

Linda (Spanish)
•beautiful

Lindsay (Scottish, English)
•camp near the stream

Linette (Welsh, French)
•idol, bird

Ling (Chinese)
•delicate, dainty

Linnea (Scandinavian)
•lime tree

Lisa (Hebrew)
•consecrated to God

Lisha (Arabic)
•darkness before midnight

Litonya (Moquelumnan)
•darting hummingbird

Livia (Hebrew)
•crown

Lois (Greek, German)
•the better, famous warrior

Lokelani (Hawaiian)
•heavenly rose

Lolita (Spanish)
•sorrowful

Lona (Latin, English)
•lioness, solitary

Lorelei (Teutonic)
•temptress

Loris (Latin, Dutch)
•thong, clown

Lorraine (Teutonic, Latin)
•famous in battle, sorrowful

Lotus (Egypt, Greek)
•bloom of forgetfulness

Louise (Teutonic)
•romantic

Love (English)
•love, kindness, charity

Luann (Hebrew, German, Hawaiian)
•graceful woman warrior

Lucerne (Latin)
•lamp, circle of light

Lucine (Arabic)
•moon

Lucretia (Latin)
•rich, rewarded

Lucy (Latin)
•light

Ludmilla (Slavonic)
•loved by the people

Lulani (Polynesian)
•highest point of heaven

Luella (Latin)
•the appeaser

Lulu (Arabic, English)
•pearl, soothing, comforting

Luna (Latin)
•the moon

Laura (Latin)
•the laurel, famous

Laurel (Latin)
•laurel tree

Lavena (Irish, French)
•joy

Laverne (French)
•springlike

Lavina (Latin)
•purified

Lavinia (Latin)
•woman of Rome

Le (Vietnamese)
•pearl

Lea (Hawaiian)
•goddess of canoe makers

Leah (Hebrew)
•the weary, wild cow

Leala (French)
•faithful, loyal

Leandra (Latin)
•like a lioness

Leda (Greek)
•lady

Lee (Anglo-Saxon, Chinese, Irish)
•meadow, plum, poetic

Leila (Aramaean, Hebrew)
•black, dark as night

Leilani (Hawaiian)
•heavenly flower, heavenly child

Lelia (Greek)
•fair speech

Lenita (Latin)
•gentle

Lenore (Greek)
•light

Leona (Latin, German)
•lion, brave as a lioness

Leora (Latin, Hebrew)
•brave as a lion, light

Leslie (Celtic)
•from the gray fort

Leta (Latin, Swahili)
•joy, delight, bringer

Letitia (Latin)
•gladness

Levanna (Hebrew, Latin)
•shining white, the moon rise

Levina (Latin)
•flash of lightning

Levona (Hebrew)
•spice, incense

Leya (Spanish, Tamil)
•loyal, the constellation Leo

Lia (Greek, Hebrew, Italian)
•bringer of good news

Liadan (Irish)
•grey lady

Lian (Chinese)
•graceful willow

Liana (Latin, French, English)
•youth, meadow

Liberty (Latin)
•free

Lida (Greek, Slavonic)
•happy, loved by people

Lien (Chinese)
•lotus

Kirima (Eskimo)
•hill

Kirsten (Scandinavian, Greek)
•the anointed one, Christian

Kirti (Marathi-Western India)
•fame

Kishi (Japanese)
•long and happy life

Kita (Japanese)
•north

Klarissa (German)
•clear, bright

Koffi (Swahili)
•born on Friday

Koko (Japanese)
•stork

Kona (Hawaiian, Hindi)
•lady, angular

Koren (Greek)
•young girl

Koto (Japanese)
•harp

Kristen (Greek)
•Christian

Kumiko (Japanese)
•girl with braids

Kuniko (Japanese)
•countryside

Kyla (Irish, Yiddish)
•attractive, crown, laurel

Kyle (Scottish)
•narrow piece of land

Kylie (West Australian)
•curled stick

Kyoko (Japanese)
•mirror

Kyra (Greek)
•lord, ladylike

Lacey (Latin)
•cheerful

Lada (Russian)
•goddess of beauty

Lakeisha (Arabic)
•woman

Lakia (Arabic)
•found treasure

Lalita (Sanskrit)
•artless

Lallie (English)
•babbler

Lana (Celtic, Latin, Hawaiian)
•handsome, wooly, floating

Lane (English)
•narrow road

Lani (Hawaiian)
•sky, heaven

Lara (Latin, Greek)
•well-known, cheerful

Larina (Greek)
•seagull

Larissa (Latin)
•laughing, cheerful

Lark (Old English)
•songbird

Latifah (Arabic, Hebrew)
•pleasant, gentle, caress

Latisha (Latin)
•joy

Keilani (Hawaiian)
•glorious chief

Keisha (African)
•favorite

Keita (Scottish)
•woods, enclosed place

Kelila (Hebrew)
•crown, laurel

Kelly (Irish)
•warrior

Kelsey (Scandinavian, Scottish)
•ship island

Kenda (Native American)
•water baby, magical power

Kendall (English)
•ruler of the valley

Kendra (Anglo-Saxon)
•the knowing woman

Kenya (Hebrew)
•animal horn

Kenzie (Scottish)
•light-skinned

Kerensa (Cornish)
•loving, affectionate

Kerry (Irish)
•dark

Kesi (Swahili)
•born during difficult time

Kessie (Ashanti)
•chubby baby

Kevyn (Irish)
•beautiful

Keziah (Hebrew)
•cinnamon-like spice

Khadijah (Arabic)
•trustworthy

Khalida (Arabic)
•immortal, everlasting

Ki (Korean)
•arisen

Kia (African)
•season's beginning

Kiara (Irish)
•little and dark

Kiaria (Japanese)
•fortunate

Kiele (Hawaiian)
•gardenia, fragrant blossom

Kiku (Japanese)
•chrysanthemum

Kiley (Irish)
•attractive, from the straits

Kim (Vietnamese)
•needle

Kimana (Native American)
•butterfly

Kimberly (Old English)
•chief, ruler

Kimi (Japanese)
•righteous

Kina (Hawaiian)
•from China

Kinsey (English)
•offspring, relative

Kioko (Japanese)
•happy child

Kiona (Native American)
•brown hills

Kira (Persian, Latin)
•sun, light

Kirby (Anglo-Saxon)
•from the church town

K

Kallan (Slavonic)
•stream, river

Kama (Sanskrit)
•loved one

Kamala (Hindi)
•lotus

Kamaria (Swahili)
•like the moon, moonlight

Kamea (Hawaiian)
•one and only, precious

Kameko (Japanese)
•turtle child

Kami (Japanese)
•divine aura

Kamilah (Arabic)
•perfect

Kanda (Native American)
•magical power

Kane (Japanese)
•two right hands

Kannitha (Cambodian)
•angel

Kanya (Hindi, Thai)
•virgin, young lady

Kapuki (Swahili)
•first-born daughter

Karen (Greek)
•pure

Karida (Arabic)
•untouched, pure

Karimah (Arabic)
•generous

Karina (Greek)
•witty

Karis (Greek)
•graceful

Karly (Latin)
•little and womanly

Karma (Hindi)
•fate, destiny, action

Kashmir (Sanskrit)
•a state in India

Kasi (Hindi)
•from the holy city

Kassidy (Irish)
•clever

Katherine (Greek)
•pure

Kaulana (Hawaiian)
•famous

Kay (Greek, Latin, Teutonic)
•rejoicing, merry

Kaya (Native American-Japanese)
•wise child, resting place

Kayla (Hebrew, Arabic)
•crown, laurel

Kayley (French)
•forest

Keara (Irish)
•dark, black

Keely (Irish)
•graceful, companion

Keena (Irish)
•brave

Kei (Japanese)
•reverent

Keiki (Hawaiian)
•child

Keiko (Japanese)
•happy child

Jolie (French)
•pretty

Jonquil (Latin, English)
•an ornamental plant

Jora (Hebrew)
•autumn rain

Jordan (Hebrew)
•descending

Jonquil (Latin, English)
•an ornamental plant with fragrant yellow flowers

Jora (Hebrew)
•autumn rain

Jordan (Hebrew)
•descending

Josephine (Hebrew, French)
•she shall add, God will add

Joshlyn (Hebrew)
•God is my salvation

Jovanna (Latin)
•majestic

Jovita (Latin)
•Jupiter, jovial

Joy (Old French, Latin)
•delight, joyous

Judith (Hebrew)
•praise of the Lord

Julie (Latin)
•youthful, downy hair

June (Latin)
•young, born in the sixth month

Junko (Japanese)
•obedient

Juno (Latin)
•queen

Justine (Latin)
•the just, righteous

Kacey (Irish)
•brave

Kachina (Native American)
•sacred dancer

Kaela (Hebrew, Arabic)
•beloved sweetheart

Kai (Hawaiian, Native American)
•sea, willow tree

Kaila (Hebrew)
•laurel, crown

Kaitlin (Irish)
•pure

Kalani (Hawaiian)
•chieftain, sky

Kalea (Hawaiian)
•bright, clear

Kalei (Hawaiian)
•flower wreath

Kalena (Hawaiian)
•pure

Kali (Sanskrit)
•dark goddess, energy

Kalila (Arabic)
•beloved

Kalina (Slavic)
•flower

Kalinda (Hindi)
•sun

Jade (Italian, Spanish)
•jade, colic

Jael (Hebrew)
•mountain goat, climber

Jamie (Hebrew, French)
•supplanting, following

Jalila (Arabic)
•great

Jamaica (Spanish)
•an island in the Caribbean

Jamila (Arabic)
•beautiful, lovely

Janan (Arabic)
•heart, soul

Jane (Hebrew)
•God is gracious

Janna (Arabic)
•harvest of fruit

Jardena (French, Spanish)
•garden

Jarita (Arabic)
•earthen water jug

Jasmine (Persian)
•a flower name

Jaspreet (Punjabi)
•virtuous

Javiera (Spanish)
•owner of a new house

Jaya (Hindi)
•victory

Jaye (Latin)
•jaybird

Jayne (Hindi)
•victorious

Jemima (Hebrew)
•dove

Jena (Arabic)
•little bird

Jennifer (Celtic)
•white wave, white phantom

Jerusha (Hebrew)
•inheritance

Jessenia (Arabic)
•flower

Jessica (Hebrew)
•grace of God, wealthy

Jesusa (Hebrew)
•God is my salvation

Jetta (English)
•jet black gem

Jewel (French)
•precious gem

Jezebel (Hebrew)
•unexalted

Jillian (Latin)
•youthful

Jimi (Hebrew)
•supplanter, substitute

Jin (Japanese)
•tender

Jina (Swahili)
•baby with a name

Joan (Hebrew)
•God's gracious gift

Jobina (Hebrew)
•the afflicted

Jocelyn (Latin)
•fair, merry

Joelle (Hebrew)
•Jehovah is the Lord

Jolene (Hebrew)
•God will add

Ignacia (Latin)
•ardent

Ilana (Hebrew)
•tree

Iliana (Greek)
•from Troy

Ima (Japanese)
•presently

Imani (Arabic)
•believer

Imelda (German)
•warrior

Imogene (Latin)
•image, likeness

Ina (Greek)
•pure

India (Sanskrit)
•river

Indigo (Latin)
•dark blue color

Indira (Hindi)
•splendid

Inez (Spanish)
•chaste

Inga (Scandinavian)
•a daughter

Ingrid (Scandinavian)
•beautiful, hero's daughter

Intisar (Arabic)
•triumph

Iola (Greek, Welsh)
•dawn, violet colored

Iona (Greek)
•purple jewel, violet flower

Iphigenia (Greek)
•sacrifice

Irene (Greek)
•peaceful

Iris (Greek)
•graceful

Irma (Teutonic)
•strong

Iruka (Nigerian)
•the future is supreme

Isadora (Greek)
•a gift

Isis (Egyptian)
•supreme goddess

Isolde (Celtic)
•fair lady

Italia (Italian)
•from Italy

Ivana (Hebrew)
•God's gracious gift

Ivory (Latin)
•made of ivory

Ivy (Old English)
•ivy

Jacinta (Greek)
•beautiful, comely

Jacobi (Hebrew)
•supplanter, substitute

Jacqueline (Hebrew)
•the supplanter

Jada (Hebrew)
•wise

Helen (Greek)
•light

Helga (Teutonic)
•holy

Helsa (Hebrew)
•given to God

Henrietta (Teutonic)
•ruler of the house

Hera (Greek)
•queen of the gods, jealous

Hermoine (Greek)
•of the earth

Hermosa (Spanish)
•beautiful

Hesper (Greek)
•evening star

Hester (Persian)
•a star

Hila (Hebrew)
•greatly praised

Hilary (Latin)
•cheerful

Hilda (Teutonic)
•strong

Hinda (Hebrew)
•hind, doe

Hiroko (Japanese)
•magnanimous

Hoa (Vietnamese)
•flower, peace

Holly (Anglo-Saxon)
•the holly

Honey (English)
•sweet

Honora (Latin)
•honorable

Hope (Anglo-Saxon)
•hope

Hortense (Latin)
•garden worker

Hoshi (Japanese)
•star

Hua (Chinese)
•flower

Huda (Arabic)
•guidance

Hyacinth (Greek)
•plant with colorful, fragrant flowers

Hye (Korean)
•graceful

Ianthe (Greek)
•delightful

Ida (Teutonic, English)
•happy, hardworking

Idelia (Teutonic)
•noble

Idola (Greek)
•vision

Idona (Teutonic)
•industrious

Iesha (Arabic)
•alive and well

Ifeoma (Ibo)
•good, beautiful

Ifetayo (Yoruba)
•love brings happiness

Gudrun (Scandinavian)
•battler

Guinevere (Celtic, French)
•fair lady, white phantom

Gwendolyn (Celtic)
•fair, new moon

Gypsy (English)
•wanderer

Habibah (Arabic)
•loved one

Hadassah (Hebrew)
•myrtle tree

Hadley (English)
•field of heather

Hagar (Hebrew)
•flight

Hagit (Hebrew)
•holiday

Haley (English, Scandinavian)
•hay clearing, heroine

Halima (Arabic, Swahili)
•gentle, patient

Halla (African)
•unexpected gift

Halona (Native American)
•fortunate

Hana (Japanese, Arabic)
•flower, happiness

Hannah (Hebrew)
•grace, compassion

Happy (English)
•happy

Harley (English)
•meadow of the hare

Harmony (Latin)
•harmony

Harpreet (Punjabi)
•devoted to God

Harriet (Teutonic, French)
•mistress of the home

Hasana (Swahili)
•she arrived first

Hasina (Swahili)
•good

Haunani (Hawaiian)
•beautiful hibiscus tree

Haviva (Hebrew)
•beloved

Hayfa (Arabic)
•shapely

Hazel (Anglo-Saxon)
•authority

Hertha (Teutonic)
•earth mother

Heather (Anglo-Saxon)
•the heather

Heaven (English)
•place of beauty and happiness

Hedda (Teutonic)
•war, battler

Hedwig (Teutonic)
•storm, strife

Hedy (Greek)
•delightful, sweet

G

Gabrielle (Hebrew)
•woman of God

Gaea (Greek)
•planet Earth

Gail (English)
•merry, lively

Galena (Greek)
•healer, calm

Galit (Hebrew)
•fountain

Garland (French)
•wreath of flowers

Garnet (Teutonic)
•radiant red jewel

Gay (French)
•merry

Gemini (Greek)
•twin

Gemma (Italian)
•gem

Gen (Japanese)
•spring

Genevieve (German, French)
•juniper tree

Georgia (Greek)
•farmer, earth-lover

Geraldine (Teutonic, German)
•affectionate, mighty

Gerda (Teutonic)
•the protected

Germaine (French)
•exquisite

Gertrude (Teutonic, German)
•beloved warrior

Gilberta (Teutonic)
•bright pledge

Gilda (Celtic, English)
•God's servant

Gin (Japanese)
•silver

Ginger (Latin)
•flower, spice

Giselle (Teutonic)
•pledge or promise

Gitana (Spanish)
•gypsy, wanderer

Gladys (Welsh, Latin, Irish)
•demure, delicate, princess

Glenna (Welsh)
•from the glen

Gloria (Latin)
•glorious

Glynis (Welsh, Scottish)
•valley, glen

Golda (English)
•gold

Grace (Latin)
•favor, grace

Greer (Greek, Scottish)
•watchwoman, vigilant

Gretchen (Greek)
•pearl

Griselda (Teutonic)
•heroine, warrior

Guadalupe (Arabic)
•river of black stones

Fabia (Latin)
•bean grower

Faith (Latin)
•faithful, believer in God

Faline (Latin)
•catlike

Fallon (Irish)
•grandchild of the ruler

Fanchon (Teutonic)
•free

Fancy (French, English)
•whimsical, decorative

Farrah (English)
•beautiful, pleasant

Faren (English)
•wanderer

Fatima (Arabic)
•daughter of the Prophet

Faustine (Latin)
•lucky

Fawn (French)
•young deer

Fay (Old French)
•fairy

Fayola (Nigerian)
•lucky

Felicia (Latin)
•happiness, lucky

Femi (French, Nigerian)
•woman, love me

Feodora (Greek)
•gift of God

Fern (Greek, English)
•feather, fern

Fernanda (German)
•daring, adventurous

Fidanka (Bulgarian)
•sapling

Fidela (Latin)
•faithful

Fiona (Celtic, Scottish)
•ivory-skinned, fair

Flair (English)
•style, verve

Flannery (Irish)
•red eyebrows, redhead

Flavia (Latin)
•blond, golden haired

Fleur (French)
•a flower

Flora (Latin)
•goddess of flowers

Florence (Latin)
•blooming, flourishing

Fonda (Spanish, Latin)
•profound, foundation, inn

Fontanna (French)
•fountain

Fontina (Teutonic)
•free

Frances (Latin, Teutonic)
•free

Freda (Teutonic)
•peace

Fredericka (Teutonic)
•peaceful

Freja (Scandinavian)
•noble-woman

E

Electra (Greek)
•shining star, brilliant

Eliana (Hebrew)
•my God has answered me

Elita (Latin, French)
•chosen

Elizabeth (Hebrew)
•promised by God

Ella (English)
•elfin, fairy-woman

Elma (Greek, Turkish)
•pleasant, sweet fruit

Eloise (Old French)
•romantic

Elsa (German)
•noble

Elvira (Spanish, Latin, German)
•like an elf, white, blond

Elysia (Latin)
•sweet, blissful

Emerald (French)
•bright green gemstone

Emily (Teutonic, Latin)
•industrious, flatterer

Emma (Teutonic)
•one who heals, universal

Emmanuelle (Hebrew)
•God is with us

Emmeline (English)
•intellectual

Endora (Hebrew)
•fountain

Erica (Scandinavian, English)
•of royalty, brave ruler

Erin (Irish)
•peace

Erina (Celtic)
•girl from Ireland

Ermine (Latin, German)
•noble, soldier

Ernestine (Teutonic)
•purposeful, earnest

Esmerelda (Greek)
•emerald

Esperanza (Spanish)
•hope

Esther (Hebrew)
•a star

Ethel (Teutonic, English)
•noble

Etta (German)
•little

Eudora (Greek)
•wonderful gift

Eugenia (Greek)
•well-born

Eulalia (Greek)
•well spoken

Eunice (Greek)
•bringing a happy victory

Euphemia (Greek)
•accomplished, famed

Eurydice (Greek)
•wide, broad

Evangeline (Greek)
•bearer of good news

Evania (Irish)
•young warrior

Eve (Hebrew)
•life, giver of life

Evelyn (Old German)
•hazelnut

Deryn (Welsh)
•bird

Desiree (French-Latin)
•hoped for

Desma (Greek)
•pledge or bond

Destiny (English, French)
•fortune, fate

Deva (Hindi)
•divine

Devin (Irish)
•poet

Diana (Latin)
•moon goddess, perfect, divine

Dinah (Hebrew)
•judgment, vindicated

Dior (French)
•golden

Dixie (French, English)
•tenth, wall, dike

Dodie (Hebrew)
•beloved

Dolores (Latin, Spanish)
•Our Lady of Sorrows

Dominique (Latin)
•born on the Lord's day

Donna (Latin)
•lady

Dora (Greek)
•gift

Doreen (Irish, French)
•moody, sullen, golden

Doris (Greek)
•sea goddess

Dorothy (Greek)
•God's gift

Drew (Greek)
•courageous, strong

Dulcie (Latin)
•sweet, charming

Dustine (German, English)
•valiant fighter, quarry

Easter (English)
•Easter time

Ebony (Greek, Middle English)
•dark wood, black

Echo (Greek)
•a Greek nymph

Edana (Celtic)
•fiery, ardent

Eden (Hebrew, Babylonian)
•delightful, enchanting

Edith (Teutonic, English)
•rich gift, stately

Edna (Greek, Hebrew)
delight, rejuvenation

Edwina (Anglo-Saxon)
•valued friend

Effie (Greek)
•fair and famed

Elaine (Greek)
•light, bright

Eldora (Spanish)
•golden, gilded

Eleanor (Greek)
•light

D

Dagny (Scandinavian)
•day

Dahlia (Scandinavian)
•valley

Dai (Japanese)
•great

Daisy (English)
•daisy, eye of the day

Dakota (Native American)
•tribal name

Dale (Teutonic)
•dweller in the valley

Dallas (Irish)
•wise

Dama (Latin)
•lady

Damica (French)
•friendly

Dana (Old English)
•from Denmark, bright as
day

Danielle (Hebrew)
•God is my Judge

Daphne (Greek)
•laurel

Dara (Hebrew)
•the heart of wisdom

Darby (Irish, Scandinavian)
•free, deer estate

Darcy (French, Irish)
•from the stronghold, dark

Darda (Hebrew)
•pearl of wisdom

Daria (Greek)
•rich

Darlene (Anglo-Saxon, French)
•dearly beloved, darling

Daryl (Old English)
•beloved, dear

Daryn (Greek, Irish)
•gifts, great

Davina (Hebrew)
•loved one

Dawn (Anglo-Saxon, English)
•break of day, sunrise

Deborah (Hebrew)
•industrious, bee

Deirdre (Irish)
•sorrowful, fear, wanderer

Deka (Somali)
•pleasing

Delana (German)
•noble protector

Delia (Greek)
•visible

Delilah (Hebrew)
•temptress, coquette

Delora (Latin)
•from the seashore

Delphine (Greek)
•calm, serene

Delta (Greek)
•door

Demetria (Greek)
•from the fertile land

Denise (Greek)
•worshipper

Derika (German)
•ruler of the people

Derry (Irish)
•redhead

Claire (Latin)
•bright, clear

Clarabelle (Latin)
•bright, shining, beautiful

Clarissa (Latin, Greek)
•making famous, brilliant

Claudia (Latin)
•dazzling, lame

Clematis (Greek)
•clinging

Clementine (Latin)
•kind, merciful

Cleopatra (Greek)
•famous

Clio (Greek)
•proclaimer, glorifier

Cloris (Greek)
•pale green

Clotilde (Teutonic)
•famous battle maiden

Clove (Old English)
•tree of the myrtle family

Clyte (Greek)
•a nymph

Coco (Spanish)
•coconut

Cody (English)
•cushion

Colby (English)
•coal town

Colette (Greek)
•victorious

Colleen (Irish)
•girl

Concetta (Italian)
•pure

Conchita (Spanish)
•conception

Concordia (Latin)
•harmonious

Constance (Latin)
•unchanging, loyal

Consuela (Latin)
•consolation

Cora (Greek)
•maiden

Coral (Latin)
•coral

Corazon (Spanish)
•heart

Cordelia (Latin, Welsh)
•sincere, sea jewel

Corinne (Greek)
•maiden

Cornelia (Latin)
•womanly virtue

Corissa (English)
•cheerful, good hearted

Courtney (Middle English)
•from the court

Crystal (Greek, Latin)
•pure, clear, brilliant glass

Cynthia (Greek)
•moon goddess

Dacey (Irish)
•southerner

Dae (English)
•day

C

Celeste (Latin)
•heavenly, celestial

Cerella (Latin)
•springtime

Cerise (French)
•cherry, cherry red

Chablis (French)
•dry white wine

Chai (Hebrew)
•life

Chalice (French)
•goblet

Chanda (Sanskrit)
•great goddess

Chandra (Sanskrit)
•she outshines the stars, moon

Chanel (French, English)
•canal, channel

Chantal (Old French)
•stone, a stony place, song

Chantilly (French)
•fine lace

Chantrea (Cambodian)
•moon, moonbeam

Chantrice (French)
•singer

Charde (Punjabi)
•charitable

Charissa (Greek)
•graceful

Charity (Latin)
•charitable, loving

Charlene (English)
•little and womanly

Charlotte (Teutonic, French)
•strong, noble-spirited

Chastity (Latin)
•sexual purity

Chava (Hebrew, Yiddish)
•life, bird

Chelsea (English)
•seaport, landing place for chalk

Cherise (French)
•grace

Cherokee (Native American)
•tribal name

Cheryl (French)
•dear one

Cheyenne (Native American)
•tribal name

Chika (Japanese)
•near and dear

China (Chinese)
•fine porcelain

Chiquita (Spanish)
•little one

Chloe (Greek)
•blossoming

Christabelle (Latin, French)
•beautiful Christian

Christine (Greek)
•fair Christian, anointed

Ciara (Irish)
•black

Cinderella (French, English)
•little cinder girl

Cindy (Greek)
•moon

Burgundy (French)
• a hearty red wine

Cachet (French)
• prestigious, desirous

Cala (Arabic)
• castle, fortress

Callie (Greek)
• most beautiful

Calandra (Greek)
• the lark

Calida (Spanish)
• warm, ardent

Calista (Greek)
• most beautiful

Camellia (Italian)
• evergreen tree or shrub

Cameron (Scottish)
• crooked nose, crooked hill

Camilla (Latin)
• noble, self-sacrificing

Candace (Latin)
• pure, glowing

Candida (Latin)
• bright white

Caprice (Italian)
• fanciful

Cara (Celtic, Latin)
• friend, dear

Carin (Latin)
• the keel

Carissa (Greek, Italian)
• grace, dear one

Carita (Latin)
• charitable

Carla (Teutonic, German)
• one who is strong, farmer

Carlin (Irish)
• little champion

Carlotta (Spanish)
• noble birth

Carmel (Hebrew)
• garden land

Carmen (Latin)
• song

Carol (Old French, English)
• song of joy, strong and womanly

Caroline (Teutonic, French)
• one who is strong, little and womanly

Caron (Welsh)
• loving, kind-hearted, charitable

Cary (Celtic)
• dark of hair or complexion

Carys (Welsh)
• love

Casey (Irish)
• watchful, brave

Cassandra (Greek)
• prophetess, helper of men

Cassia (Greek)
• spicy cinnamon

Cassidy (Irish)
• clever

Catherine (Greek)
• pure

Cecilia (Latin)
• musical, blind

B

Bertina (English)
- bright, shining

Bertha (Teutonic)
- bright, brilliant ruler

Bertilde (Teutonic)
- commanding

Beryl (Hebrew, Greek)
- jewel

Bethany (Aramaic)
- house of poverty

Beverly (Anglo-Saxon)
- beaver meadow

Bianca (Italian)
- white

Blaine (Irish)
- thin

Blair (Celtic)
- flat land

Blaise (French)
- one who stammers

Blake (English)
- dark

Blanche (Old French)
- white, fair

Blenda (Teutonic)
- dazzling, glorious

Bliss (Old English)
- intense happiness

Blondie (English)
- blond

Blossom (Old English)
- flower of a plant

Blythe (Anglo-Saxon)
- happy, joyous

Bo (Chinese)
- precious

Bonnie (Old English)
- pretty, sweet

Bonita (Spanish)
- pretty

Brandy (Dutch)
- burnt wine

Breck (Irish)
- freckled

Bree (English)
- broth

Breena (Irish)
- fairy place

Brenda (Irish, English)
- fiery, little raven, sword

Brenna (Celtic)
- maiden with raven hair

Briana (Celtic, Irish)
- strong, virtuous, honorable

Briar (French)
- heather

Bridget (Celtic, Irish)
- strong

Brie (French)
- a type of cheese

Brisa (Spanish)
- beloved

Brittany (French, English)
- from Britain

Brooke (Old English)
- brook, stream

Brynn (Welsh, Latin)
- hill, boundary line

Buffy (American)
- buffalo, from the plains

Bunny (English)
- little rabbit

Aspen (Old English)
•the tree

Astra (Greek)
•like a star

Astrid (Scandinavian)
•beautiful, as a goddess

Atalie (Swiss)
•pure

Athena (Greek)
•wisdom

Atifa (Arabic)
•affection

Aubrey (Teutonic)
•ruler of the elves

Audra (Lithuanian)
•thunderstorm

Audrey (Old English)
•noble strength

Augusta (Latin)
•majestic, exalted

Aurelia (Latin)
•golden

Aurora (Latin)
•dawn

Autumn (Latin)
•the season

Ava (Hebrew)
•life

Avis (Latin)
•bird

Ayanna (Hindi)
•innocent

Ayla (Hebrew)
•oak tree

Azalia (Hebrew)
•whom God has spared

B

Bailey (Old French)
•manager, local official

Bambi (Italian)
•child

Barbara (Greek)
•mysterious, foreign

Barrie (Irish)
•spear

Basia (Hebrew)
•daughter of God

Beata (Latin)
•blessed

Beatrice (Latin)
•she brings joy

Bela (Czech)
•white

Belicia (Spanish)
•dedicated to God

Belinda (English, Spanish)
•shining, bright, beautiful

Belle (Latin, French)
•beautiful

Belva (Latin)
•beautiful view

Bena (Hebrew)
•wise

Bernadette (Teutonic)
•brave, strong

Bernadine (German)
•brave as a bear

Bernice (Greek)
•bringing victory

A

Anastasia (Greek)
•one who will rise again

Anatola (Greek)
•of the east

Andrea (Greek, Latin)
•strong, feminine

Anela (Hawaiian)
•angel

Angela (Greek)
•angel, heavenly

Angelina (Greek)
•messenger

Anika (African)
•sweetness of face

Ann (Hebrew)
•full of grace

Annabel (Latin)
•graceful, beautiful

Annelise (German)
•blend of Anne and Elise

Anselma (Teutonic)
•protectress

Ansley (Old English)
•hermitage in the woods

Anthea (Greek)
•like a flower

Antonia (Greek, Latin)
•flourishing, praiseworthy

Aphrodite (Greek)
•goddess of Love

April (Latin)
•to open, early spring

Arabella (Latin)
•fair, beautiful

Ardelle (Latin)
•enthusiastic, warm

Arden (English)
•valley of the eagle, romantic refuge

Ardith (Hebrew)
•rich gift

Ardra (Latin)
•fervent, eager

Aretha (Greek)
•virtuous

Ariadne (Greek)
•holy one

Ariana (Celtic)
•silvery

Arica (Scandinavian)
•ruler of all

Ariel (Hebrew)
•lioness of God

Arin (Hebrew)
•enlightened

Arlene (Celtic)
•a pledge

Artha (Hindi)
•wealthy

Artis (Irish)
•noble, lofty hill

Ashley (American from Irish)
•of ash tree meadow

Asia (Greek)
•the continent

A

Alfreda (Teutonic)
•supernaturally wise

Alice (Greek)
•truthful, noble

Alida (Latin)
•small, winged one

Alika (Hawaiian, Swahili)
•truthful, most beautiful

Alina (Old German)
•of noble kind

Alisa (Hebrew)
•great happiness

Alisha (Greek)
•truthful

Aliza (Hebrew)
•joyful

Allegra (Latin)
•cheerful

Alma (Latin)
•cherishing

Almira (Arabic)
•princess

Aloyse (Teutonic)
•famous in battle

Althea (Greek)
•wholesome, healing

Alva (Latin)
•white

Alvina (Teutonic)
•beloved, friend of all

Alvita (Latin)
•vivacious

Alyssa (Greek)
•rational

Ama (African)
•born on Saturday

Amabel (Latin)
•lovable

Amada (Spanish)
•beloved

Amal (Arabic)
•hopeful

Amanda (Latin)
•worthy to be loved

Amara (Greek)
•unfading

Amaris (Hebrew)
•whom God has promised

Amaryllis (Greek)
•fresh, sparkling

Amaya (Japanese)
•night rain

Amber (Arabic)
•a jewel

Amberly (Old English)
•a place in England

Amelia (Teutonic)
•industrious

Amena (Celtic)
•honest

Amethyst (Greek)
•the semiprecious stone, sober

Amity (Latin)
•friendly

Amy (Latin)
•beloved

Ananda (Hindi)
•blissful

A

Abigail (Teutonic)
•source of joy

Abra (Hebrew)
•mother of many nations

Adabel (Teutonic)
•happy and fair

Adara (Greek, Arabic)
•beauty, virgin

Adele (Teutonic)
•of noble rank

Adena (Greek, Hebrew)
•noble, adorned

Adiel (Teutonic)
•ornament of God

Adora (Teutonic)
•the beloved

Adria (Latin)
•the unknown

Adrienne (Latin)
•woman of the sea

Afton (English)
•place in England

Agate (English)
•the semiprecious stone

Agatha (Greek)
•good

Agnes (Greek)
•pure, chaste

Ahava (Hebrew)
•beloved

Aiko (Japanese)
•beloved

Aileen (Greek)
•light

Ailsa (Teutonic)
•of good cheer

Aimee (French)
•beloved

Ainsley (Scottish)
•my own meadow

Airlia (Greek)
•ethereal

Alameda (Spanish)
•the poplar tree

Alana (Celtic)
•fair, comely

Alba (Latin)
•the Italian city on a white hill

Alberta (Teutonic)
•noble, brilliant

Alcina (Greek)
•strong-minded

Alda (Teutonic)
•rich

Aldis (Old English)
•from the house

Aldora (Greek)
•winged gift

Alea (Arabic)
•high, exalted

Alethea (Greek)
•truth

Alexandra (Greek)
•defender of mankind

Alexis (Greek)
•helper

name that

BABY
GIRL

over 3000 names
and their meanings
for your baby

written by Joan Verniero
illustrated by Kerren Barbas

The C.R.Gibson Company, Norwalk, Connecticut 06856

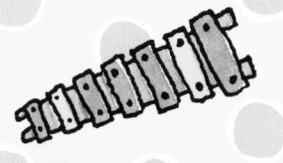
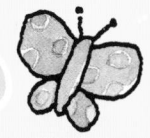

Choosing the perfect name for your infant can be a joyous experience for you. Today's children are named after people, animals, flowers, minerals and even planets and stars. Few will criticize if you just make up a name! Look at the choices you have for every letter!

On the other hand, the whole exercise may be too huge, and you may be having trouble narrowing down those choices. "My daughter has to live with this name for a long time." "I don't want my child to hate her name." "But I want it to be meaningful." You may be thinking some or all of these things.

Name That Baby Girl is designed as an easy-to-use reality check to help you choose that perfect name for your perfect baby. Traditional names, unusual names, the most popular names, international names and legendary and mythical names —you'll find a melting pot of possibilities. Each name appears with its place of origin and its meaning. When a name draws from several countries, as many do, the various cultures are noted, and the meaning given reflects the standard meaning.

Don't despair if you have what you consider a simple name in mind, and you can't find it. The range of names is narrowed to include only one of the variety of names taken from the same root. For example, Adele, of noble rank and Teutonic origin, was chosen to represent the family of names including Adela and Adelaide. The Where to Find list below will assist you in finding other popular names.

Where to Find ...

Bess, Betsy, Betty, Beth, Bettina	see Elizabeth
Cathleen, Kathleen	see Catherine, Katherine
Ellen	see Helen
Isabel(le), Isobel	see Elizabeth
Jean, Jeannette	see Joan
Mara, Marie, Maria, Marilyn, Marion	see Mary

Most of all, trust yourself to choose that perfect name for that perfect little girl!

—Joan C. Verniero